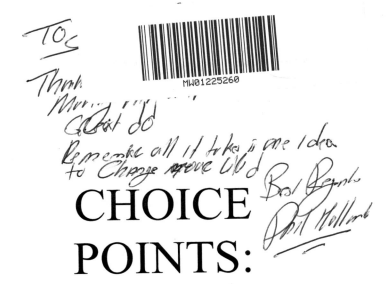

To

Think

About do

Remember all it takes is one idea
to change your Life

(signatures)

CHOICE
POINTS:

When You Have to Decide
Which Way to Go

DEDICATIONS

To my father, Paul Hollander, who inspired me with his passion for lifelong learning; to my great aunt Adelene who lived these principles her whole life; and to my beautiful wife Lisa and two wonderful children Sydney and Ryan whom I sincerely wish to inspire to take the ideas contained in this book and make them their own.

- **Phil Hollander**

To the most loving, supportive, and understanding wife anyone could ask for, (and a terrific editor), Margaret Whelan.

- **Bob Reaume**

To acknowledge the life changing philosophy and skills I have acquired by studying and applying the insights and theories of two of the most eminent psychologists of the last century, Dr. Albert Ellis and Dr. Wayne Dyer. I could never have contributed to this book without them. As well, I sincerely believe that my wife and family, along with the students and clients I have taught and counselled over many years, have also been significantly enriched by these concepts and values. I am, therefore, quite confident that you, dear reader, will also derive similar important benefits.

- **Harvey Silver**

CHOICE POINTS:

When You Have to Decide Which Way to Go

Phil Hollander

Robert Reaume

Harvey Silver

Published by

Hollander, Reaume, Silver

Choice Points

Copyright © 2013

Cover design, Ana Botelho
Copyright © 2013

Published by Hollander, Reaume, Silver

Manufactured in the U.S.A.
Published in Canada

Second Edition 2013

ISBN: 978-0-9881227-0-3

Why We Wrote This Book

Nobody can go back in time to start a new beginning to their life, but every person can start today to create and develop a new ending.

Every day of your life you are confronted with having to make decisions and take actions. Some of the choices lead to disappointment or failure, while other decisions will lead to satisfaction and success. Your goals and the choices you make concerning how you think about yourself, the relationships you have with other people, and how you choose to deal with the various situations and circumstances you encounter in your daily existence will significantly determine the quality of your life.

Although you have the freedom to make your daily choices, you don't have the power to choose and control the results of your decisions and actions. After your choice is made, the consequences are now beyond your influence.

While your parents are responsible for giving you birth, only you are personally responsible for the choices you make to give meaning to your life. These choices are influenced by your beliefs and values, your view of your place in the world, the ideas put forward by people you respect, your personal objectives, and a host of other factors which are unique for each individual.

This book represents a collection of concepts, principles, and ideas that are designed to help you think more rationally about many areas of your life so you will become more competent in making wiser choices as you grow and evolve. It can provide you with guidance and a more objective perspective to help you make up your mind when you have to decide which way to go.

Some of these ideas will confirm and validate the choices you have already made or intend to make. Other concepts will challenge you to re-consider your decisions and perhaps change the path you are now planning to follow. And finally, some of these ideas will stimulate you to consider brand new options or choices which you had never previously considered.

We hope you enjoy reading this book and reflect on the diverse ideas which are contained in its pages. If it makes you stop occasionally and say to yourself, "Hmm, that makes sense," then that's a first good step. If you have an 'Aha!' moment, and believe the point is a real quality idea—a 'choice point'—then you are definitely making progress. But most importantly, if after reading this book you decide to turn off the auto-pilot and cruise control, and incorporate some of these Choice Points as deliberate habits in your life, then your path to increased life satisfaction and success will be almost guaranteed.

This book can help you do all that.

Acknowledgment: Inspirational quotes form part of our ability to frame thought and discussion. Where possible, we have noted the authors of quotes we have used. To those anonymous authors of some of the most common expressions, we thank you.

Table of Contents

1. First, Awareness:

A PERSON WHO IS UNAWARE, IS UNAWARE THAT THEY ARE UNAWARE.

A person doesn't know what they don't know. Someone who is unaware is not aware that they are unaware.

What causes 'unawareness'? Try picturing yourself holding your hands directly in front of your eyes. With your vision being blocked by your hand, it's impossible to see another person, a building, or even a mountain.

In other words, when you are too close to yourself, when you are too hung up by your own ego, biases, pride, feelings, and the emotions of self-interest, you create a blind spot or barrier to awareness. This blind spot makes it impossible to objectively assess yourself or your own performance. It results in being defensive and perhaps unreceptive to feedback. The old expression applies here:

"There are none so blind as those who will not see!"

Being unaware, unfortunately, leads to ignorance. Without true objective knowledge of ourselves, we cannot see beyond the blind spot. This ignorance, caused by unawareness, can lead us to resist information that we don't wish to receive, even though it may be useful information.

In a world that is continuously changing, refusing to move beyond our own comfort zone, and carrying on solely with previous habits and actions, will prevent us from progressing. To meet current and future challenges, we must become aware of our blind spots and areas of ignorance, and assess ourselves more objectively.

Without awareness, we are destined to repeat our past behaviour. However, change and improvement can begin when we learn how to receive and accept feedback.

If learners are receptive to feedback, they can move from unawareness to awareness, an essential first step, a giant step, toward improving their lives.

2. Chains of Belief:

PEOPLE DO NOT ATTEMPT THINGS THEY BELIEVE THEY CANNOT ACHIEVE, AND SO THEY SELDOM ACHIEVE MORE THAN THEY THINK THEY CAN.

At the circus, when a baby elephant is born, the trainer attaches a chain or thick rope to one of its legs and connects the other end to a stake in the ground. The animal moves around, but is limited in its freedom and mobility by the length of the restraining device. Four years later, when the elephant is a mature adult weighing somewhere between eight and ten thousand pounds, it still travels only as far as the chain permits. And yet in their natural habitat in India or Africa, adult elephants can literally push over or pull up trees with the massive strength they possess.

This conditioning process, starting at a very early age, has taught the elephant that the chain on its leg is so strong that escape is impossible.

In reality, it's the chain in its mind, rather than the chain on its leg, that actually limits the elephant's freedom.

Henry Ford expressed this concept quite well when he said: "If you think you can, or can't, you're right!" Most of our barriers are mental or psychological, rather than physical. Prior to the mid 1950's, it was thought to be impossible for a human being to run a mile in under 4 minutes. It had never been done. And then in 1954, a sprinter from England, Roger Bannister, broke the 4-minute mile barrier. Soon thereafter, a few other runners were able to repeat this feat. Today, over 500 runners have broken the 4-minute mile barrier.

A mile is still 5,280 feet. What is different? It's the belief that human beings, with sufficient training and skill, can break a barrier that was thought to be physically impossible to break.

All of us have some chains that shackle our minds. We all have self-defeating beliefs and irrational fears that limit what we say or do. "The wish is father to the deed," is a wise proverb. In other words, our thoughts lead to actions. If we can't think it, we will not even try to do it.

All of us are chronic underachievers. Nobody ever dies from over-thinking. When we change how and what we think, we can break the mental chains and eliminate the self-doubts that limit us. At that point, we can aim for new heights of accomplishment. There may be practical limits to our knowledge, but our imagination is infinite in scope when there are no restraining psychological chains that prevent us from realizing our potential.

3. Working for You:

PSYCHOLOGICALLY, YOU ARE AN INDEPENDENT CONTRACTOR AND YOU WORK FOR YOURSELF.

Your place of employment is generally represented by the organization's name and its location. The one to whom you report is usually your boss, the person on the organizational chart above you. But, the person you work for ... is you! You are responsible for quenching your thirst when you are thirsty because nobody else can drink for you. When you are hungry, you are responsible for eating. When you need oxygen, you breathe.

By acknowledging that you work for yourself, you are accepting the concept that you are accountable and responsible for your own morale, happiness, and general level of job satisfaction.

Even if you have a full-time job, you are still an independent contractor. You are selling your time and services to the organization you believe will give you some measure of fulfillment, and that you will earn a level of compensation that enables you to meet your personal and/or family requirements. In today's marketplace, the concept of entitlement or lifetime job security is simply not sustainable.

Organizations may give people jobs, but individuals who are offered jobs have to choose to accept them, or not. What organizations are really doing is providing an opportunity, and it is up to the individual to seize that opportunity and exploit it, if that's what they wish to do. If you are no longer able to add value, or if you fail to meet the needs of your company, you will likely be asked to change, improve, or move out. Similarly, if the organization fails to meet your needs and career aspirations, you can choose to move on, although some people choose to remain in jobs that they find unfulfilling and unrewarding.

Realizing that you are essentially self-employed provides you with a heightened sense of responsibility, freedom, professionalism, fulfillment, and personal empowerment. It puts you in the driver's seat of your career.

4. Taking Direct Responsibility For Your Learning:

LEARNING HOW TO LEARN IS ONE OF THE MOST IMPORTANT LIFE SKILLS.

Whether we are aware of it or not, each one of us has a unique way we like to process and filter information from the outside world. Each of us has a special way we like to learn. Information from the outside world is presented in a variety of different forms. The first way we filter this information is through our five senses: sight, sound, feeling, taste, and smell. If you think about it, you will see that your brain is performing one of, or a combination of, the following six functions at any time. You are seeing images, hearing sounds, experiencing feelings, smelling, tasting, and/or talking to yourself (or thinking) about what you are experiencing.

If you doubt this, stop right now and check your internal experience. You will become tuned into the fact that it is so. However, most of us, whether we are conscious of the fact or not, have a dominant sense that we rely on to process information from the outside world. Some of us have a preference for learning visually. Others like to process information auditorily. Some still process by doing and feeling. In samplings of participants in typical learning environments, approximately 40% of the population prefers to learn information visually; 40% have a preference for learning information kinesthetically, or through doing and feeling; and 20% of the population likes to learn auditorily, or through hearing.

When it comes to learning, the challenge for most of us is that information is not always presented to us in the way we prefer to receive it or in accordance with our dominant learning sensory preference. This presents problems for many people. For instance, someone with a preference for auditory learning may communicate ideas to others through words alone. This may be unpalatable to a visual learner who best understands pictures and diagrams. It may be even less effective to the kinesthetic learner who learns best through doing.

Given that information from the outside world is often presented to us in ways that differ from how we would best like to learn, it is imperative that we take an active, not a passive, role in how we learn. Taking responsibility for your learning means that you have to learn and develop strategies to convert information so it best fits your dominant learning preference. Some accelerated learning methodologies have been developed that will greatly assist you in doing just that. Learning how to learn is one of the most important life skills you could possibly learn. By doing so, you open up a world of knowledge that you may have otherwise ignored because it was not presented to you in just the right way. By taking direct responsibility for your learning, you go from being a passive recipient of information to becoming an active life-long learner.

5. Your Beliefs:

YOUR BELIEFS DETERMINE YOUR SUCCESS.

It has often been observed that we do not actually see with our eyes, but rather with our brain. It is true that our eyes are the primary means through which an external stimulus enters our perceptual awareness. But one of the primary ways we filter and process this information in our brain is through our beliefs.

Our beliefs are one of the major factors that determine whether you are successful in life. These include beliefs about your abilities, what is possible and what is not, and about the nature of reality itself. You could have abundant knowledge, talent, and skills in any particular area, but if you lack fundamental beliefs in yourself and your abilities, or if you don't believe that what you want to accomplish is possible, there is a low probability that you will succeed. In fact, if your beliefs are not in alignment with what you want to accomplish, in all probability, you won't attempt to accomplish what you want. You won't set as a goal something that otherwise could be easily obtainable.

Our beliefs about ourselves and our abilities are typically developed in our formative years by the experiences that we have, our parents, the school system, the religion that we ascribe to and the culture and society in which we live. Buckminster Fuller once stated: "I am convinced all of humanity is born with more gifts than we know. Most are born geniuses and just get degeniused rapidly."

Some of our beliefs help us, support us, and contribute to our success and the attainment of our life goals; others get in the way and often stop us in our tracks. Many of our beliefs are unconscious. They are there, but we are not aware that they exist.

Too often, we simply think the person who has obtained what we want is superior, is more talented in some way, has had better opportunities or a better childhood, or has been blessed with good fortune. The difference between someone who is successful in a given area and someone who is not may simply be the differences in their beliefs and how these differences manifest themselves in the actions the two individuals take.

Just because we have certain beliefs, whether we are conscious of them or not, does not mean that they are true. They are simply beliefs we hold for various reasons. The good news is that they can be changed. Since we have adopted them in the first place we can, if we choose, change them. So, how do you change a limiting belief and transform it into an empowering belief that supports you in the attainment of your goals?

The first step, after recognizing that you may have limiting beliefs in the first place, is to question their validity. Beliefs are essentially generalizations about the way things are. As with most generalizations, all it takes is one exception to prove that the belief that you have may have been built on a faulty premise. As you examine your beliefs, in relation to what you want to accomplish in life, ask yourself this: Are my beliefs supportive and in alignment with the attainment of my goals?

You job is to determine if there are different, more beneficial, beliefs that you can adopt about yourself and your abilities. Do those people who have obtained your desired outcome hold similar or different beliefs than you? If different, what are the beliefs that they have? How can you learn to make such beliefs yours?

Challenging your current beliefs and adopting new, more empowering beliefs involves taking a risk. You have to challenge your current way of thinking and change the way that you behave so that your behaviour is in alignment with your new beliefs. This often means stepping out of our comfort zone and stepping into the unknown. Once we overcome the fear associated with changing our behaviour, even though we don't know what the results will be, we may be pleasantly surprised by what we can accomplish. In addition, our new behaviour and the new results that we achieve will reinforce our new beliefs. These behaviours and results will support and encourage even more success in the future. Hence, you begin an upward spiral of success and accomplishment, all hinged on becoming aware of and modifying your beliefs.

Our world, indeed our entire life itself, is defined by our beliefs. Rather than being defined and limited by the beliefs of others, define for yourself what you want and what is possible for you to achieve. Challenge your current beliefs, identify, and adopt the beliefs of those who have accomplished what you want. Take back control of one of the major forces that shape your life experience, and ultimately create a better life as a result of revising your previous beliefs and values.

Whatever your desired outcomes are in life, the following is a list of some beliefs that you may choose to adopt which will serve to positively enhance your overall life experience:

- *Whatever you think you are, you are more than that.*

- *We live in an abundant universe with infinite possibilities.*

- *If even one other person has accomplished something, then it is possible for you to do so.*

- *You have more talent and skills than you could possibly use or access in a lifetime.*

- *The knowledge and skills you have developed in one area of your life is evidence that you can be equally knowledgeable and talented, or even more so, in another area.*

Choice Points

- *You are one hundred percent responsible for the results that you create in your life. You are "a cause of" instead of "an effect of" your life circumstances.*

- *You can create a better future today through changing the way you think, feel, and behave.*

- *You are in charge of your thinking; therefore, you are in charge of your results.*

- *The past does not equal the future.*

- *There is no failure, only feedback.*

- *You have the ability to learn, adapt, grow, be, do, and have more than you have ever had before.*

- *For life to get better, you must get better.*

- *You have the power to choose the beliefs that positively support what you want in your life.*

- *Your best days are yet to come!*

Try this Belief Exercise:

1. Identify three major goals that you want to accomplish in your life.

2. Ask yourself, what are some of the beliefs you currently have about your ability to accomplish these goals.

3. What beliefs would serve to make the obtainment of these goals easier and more certain?

6. Your Values:

A POWERFUL FORCE THAT SHAPES AND DEFINES YOUR LIFE.

One of the most powerful forces that shapes and defines who you are as a person is your values. Values are what you consider important in life. They are the conscious and unconscious rules that govern your life and, as a direct consequence, play a major role in determining your behaviour or what you will do or not do in any given situation.

You have different values for all aspects of your life. You have values for your health, your relationships, finances, work or career, and pretty much every other aspect of your life.

As with beliefs, our values are largely formed early on in life by our parents, education, our religion, the society or culture we live in, and by our life experiences. Our values are not static. They change and evolve through-out our lifetime as we mature and grow. At one point in your life, the acquisition of money and material possessions may be the most important value for you; however, this can change dramatically if you were to encounter a major health concern that forced you to pay more attention to your health and wellbeing instead of the next major business or career milestone. Some people change their values significantly once they have a family. People may change their values if they find their lives have become unbalanced in one area. This might cause them to re-evaluate how they have been living and to place more value or importance on another area that has been neglected.

Whether you are aware of it or not, you have what is called a values hierarchy. This is the order of importance in which we place the values we have for each major area of our life. For example, you may value family more than your career and your career more than your health and so on. Why is this important to know? This is of great significance in our lives because our dominant, or most important, values will ultimately determine what we will or will not do in a given situation—especially given the choice between two competing options. In short, your values drive both the decisions that you make and your behaviour. As a direct consequence, values are a powerful force that shape and define your life experience.

As an illustration of how your values play a significant role in determining your behaviour, imagine a situation where you are at work and your boss or client asks if you would stay late to finish a project you are working on. Due to changing circumstances, it needs to be completed ahead of the original deadline. This may not be a problem in most instances; however, this particular evening is your daughter's dance recital and you had promised her that you would be there for her big night. What do you do? Ultimately, your decision to stay at work or to go to your daughter's dance recital will be determined by what you value most.

Let's say you stay at work. This decision may not be based on you valuing your career over your daughter. You may fear losing your job if you don't stay. And if you lose your job, you may not be able to provide for your family, so the value of being able to provide for your family may cause you to skip something that is important to you. You may value your daughter over your job, but you value providing for your family over one dance recital, albeit an important event. So, as you can see, a complex set of values can influence the choices we make.

Here is another example to consider. You are on the way to the gym to work out and a friend calls and says that they have two tickets to the baseball game. Again, what you decide will largely be based on what you value most at that point in your life. In this instance, it could be fitness versus friendship, or fitness versus entertainment. Whenever two of our values conflict, our dominant value, or what we consider the most important one, usually wins the day.

Want to know what your major values are? Simply look at how you spend your time. Since our values drive our behaviour, take a good look at how and what you spend the majority of your time doing. That will help you gain insight into your value system.

Another sure indicator of what your dominant values are is to take a look at your long-term relationships. It is easier to foster friendships or long-term relationships when you share similar values in the major areas of life. So, look at the values of the people closest to you, and you should gain some insight into your own values.

If you are unbalanced in any area of your life, it may be time for values realignment. Generally, we are healthiest and happiest when all the major areas of our lives are in harmony with respect to one another. If you are spending too much time and energy in one area at the expense of another, this can have major consequences in your life. If you value the pursuit of money, for example, over your relationships with others, or taking care of your health, you will find yourself with solid financial resources, but fewer friends and poorer health to enjoy the fruits of your labour.

You can consciously choose to change your values—often quite dramatically. At times, external circumstances might influence a change in values. For instance, if your doctor tells you that you are at risk of developing heart disease if you do not take better care of yourself, this can motivate you to value your health more than you had previously.

The good news is that you can also consciously choose to change your values hierarchy without being pushed to the wall by external circumstances.

How do you do this? The first step is to identify your most important values. Examining your current behaviour is one way to get a fix on your current values. The next step is to identify which values you have neglected and need to elevate in terms of importance. Once you know where you are relative to where you want to be, the final step is to identify compelling reasons why your desired values are important to you. This involves identifying the positive benefits of adopting the new value as well as the consequences of not doing so.

For example, if you want to value your health more than you do, list the benefits of why regular exercise is important to you. Then, make a list of the consequences of not exercising regularly and of not eating well. In short, you have to use both the "carrot" and the "stick" on yourself if you want to change values. You can also apply this same methodology to values on which you currently place too much importance. For instance, if you are a workaholic, ask yourself what the benefits of working less will be, and what the consequences of not working less will be. In this way, you can bring greater harmony and balance to your life.

Once again, the primary reason why your values are so important is that they play such a powerful role in shaping your behavior and, indeed, your entire life.

7. Your Talent:

"YOUR TALENT IS GOD'S GIFT TO YOU. WHAT YOU DO WITH IT IS YOUR GIFT BACK TO GOD."
– *Robert Browning*

Almost all of us were born with virtually unlimited potential. Whether we are consciously aware of it or not, each one of us has vast reservoirs of knowledge, talents, skills, and abilities that lay dormant within—until they are tapped into by either our intent or by circumstance.

We were born with talents and abilities, and it is our responsibility to develop and express these talents for the service and betterment of humanity. To not do so not only limits the individual, it also has an impact on all of us, since we are all interconnected at some level. The challenge for most of us is that, while we have this great potential, it has often been negatively influenced by a variety of factors: well-meaning parents, the educational system, and often by society as a whole. The consequence is that most of us have adopted limiting beliefs about ourselves and our capabilities.

One of the greatest challenges we face in life, beyond discovering our supreme talents, is to nurture and enhance them in the service of others. Once we discover and apply this truth in our lives, we can begin to realize and live our life's purpose. It is then that our lives have meaning and direction and we find our enjoyment of life at its peak.

8. Nothing Happens by Accident:

ALL BEHAVIOUR IS MEANINGFUL.

Everything we say or do has a purpose and reason behind it. All of our actions are goal-oriented and are based on satisfying our needs.

We have six basic NEEDS:

1) Air

2) Water

3) Food

4) Shelter or protection against harsh weather

5) Elimination of the body's waste products

6) Sleep.

Human beings, like animals, will die if any one of these six basic needs is not met. Except in some rare cases, human beings don't need a doctor or therapist to tell them to fulfill their basic needs.

We also have five basic WANTS, DESIRES or PREFERENCES:

1) To be healthy, live, thrive, survive, and simply exist;

2) To maximize our pleasure, ease and comfort, and minimize our pain, inconveniences and discomfort;

3) To feel that we are important and respected, and acknowledged as having special value and significance, which manifests itself as a desire to be praised, recognized, and appreciated, and to have some sense of power, status, and influence;

4) To have somebody care about us, want to spend time with us, and show us affection and love;

5) To have something new and different, so we will have some variety in our lives that will reduce, or eliminate, monotony and boredom.

If our needs are not satisfied, we will eventually die because we cannot continue living when there is extreme deprivation of these physical, life-sustaining requirements.

On the other hand, if our wants or desires are not met, our satisfaction in life is diminished.

However, if our dissatisfaction is significant, we can develop thoughts that produce feelings of disappointment, regret, anxiety, hopelessness, unhappiness, frustration, anger, self-pity, and other negative emotions. These feelings of discomfort and distress can cause people to abuse alcohol or drugs or pursue other addictions. In addition, they may cause people to seek professional therapeutic assistance as a method to cope with what we perceive as psychological deprivation.

In extreme cases, these dysfunctional thoughts and feelings can lead to suicide, a permanent solution to some of life's often temporary problems. If we blame others for our psychological discomfort, such thoughts, in extreme circumstances, can lead to homicide, which is also a permanent solution to a problem that, by definition, is only temporary.

This confusion between our NEEDS and WANTS, and placing our desires into the same category as our life-sustaining physical requirements, unfortunately produces many of the stories that make the headlines in our daily media.

Thinking rationally, rather than emotionally, would contribute significantly to the reduction of these unfortunate and preventable life experiences. But that requires an awareness of, and change in, our beliefs, values, and ways of thinking.

9. Choose Your Thoughts Wisely:

HAPPINESS OR MISERY IS PRIMARILY A MATTER OF PERCEPTION AND CHOICE.

In his most famous drama, *Hamlet,* Shakespeare wrote, "Nothing is either good or bad, but thinking makes it so." The English poet, John Milton, observed, "The mind is a special place, and in itself, it can make a heaven out of hell or a hell out of heaven."

To a farmer, rain during a drought is great news. To a couple being married outdoors, however, rain is terrible news. The same event or stimulus can evoke very different reactions, depending on your mindset, and point of view, and objectives.

Let's face it, many of life's events are not within our control. But our reactions, which are generally emotional, or our responses, which are generally rational, to those events—how we choose to think, feel and behave—are totally within our control. This means that we can actually influence and control our thoughts when we set our mind to this important task.

Feelings arise as a result of our thoughts or beliefs about ourselves, other people, or a specific situation or event. Emotions, therefore, are not the cause of our thoughts; they are a by-product, result, or the consequence, of our thinking. We can influence and decide how we wish to feel, and then choose the thoughts and behaviours that will help us achieve our objective. We can eliminate any emotion with which we are uncomfortable simply by changing how we think or re-evaluating a situation or person that we originally perceived of as negative.

As Dr. Wayne Dyer wrote, "If you change the way you look at things, the things you look at change." As a result, the feelings of anxiety, anger, and self-pity, all of which can ruin careers, families, and lives, really are optional and not predetermined or outside of our conscious control.

So why choose to be miserable when the alternative is so much more satisfying? Building bridges is more productive than erecting walls. And it only takes as long as it takes to think a different thought! When you control how and what you think, then you are truly in the driver's seat of your life!

10. Controlling Goals:

A. THE PERSON WITH THE GOAL IS ALWAYS IN CONTROL.

B. THOSE WHO DON'T HAVE GOALS WILL ALWAYS BE LED AROUND BY THOSE WHO DO.

A flowing river without large banks of earth and rock on each side becomes a great big puddle or stagnant pond. Similarly, behaviour without goals to guide or direct one's actions is like having a high pressure hose with nobody there to aim it. The water simply sprays all over the place.

Goals provide direction, guidance, and the energy to initiate actions, which will help you achieve your objectives. Adrenalin is released by the brain in emergency situations. For example, if somebody is pinned under a vehicle, the rush of adrenalin gives the rescuer immense strength that can be used to help him free the accident victim. An important, clear, specific goal, to which one is committed, releases energy that normally is not called upon. In a less dramatic example, try to recall how much energy you had and how much you accomplished on the last day before you took a two week vacation. Our productivity is significantly higher because of the importance of the deadline and the clarity of our goals.

If you are driving without a specific destination, you will likely waste a lot of energy, and gas in this instance, as you wander up and down a variety of streets. And where you'll end up is anybody's guess. If you don't know where you want to go, then any road will take you there!

People with clear goals generally accomplish more, emerge as leaders, and attract others to join them. When you are focused in your own mind about what needs to be accomplished, why this objective is important, and how it can be achieved, you will be more skillful in communicating this information with enthusiasm so that others understand and willingly join in with you. Once that occurs, you will have a committed team pulling together to achieve this mutually beneficial objective.

Choice Points

Animals rely on instincts to guide their behaviour. Human beings require clear goals to help them behave efficiently and effectively.

11. Heredity Plus Learning:

YOUR PARENTS ARE
RESPONSIBLE FOR THE
FEATURES OF YOUR FACE, BUT
YOU ARE RESPONSIBLE FOR
THE EXPRESSION ON IT.
- *Anonymous*

Our 46 chromosomes and approximately 30,000 genes which we inherited from our parents determine the looks and appearance we were born with. The colour of our hair, skin and eyes, the shape of our chin, the contours of our nose, the puffiness of our cheeks or lips, our height and general shape of our body, and so on.

We can brag or complain about what nature has provided but, apart from cosmetic surgery, we are stuck with what we have inherited.

However, your smile, frown, or pouting expression is controlled by you. The tone of your voice—monotone, excited, whisper—is the result of how you choose to play your two vocal chords which is your 'musical in-strument' for making sound. In other words, you can choose to look and sound happy, bored, angry, friendly, confident, sullen, exhilarated, etc.

Our thoughts and feelings, which originate in the mind, influence and determine how we appear to other people. Controlling thoughts and feelings, and using them to convey specific looks, emotions and sounds is what actors do when they portray characters in plays, TV shows or movies.

Think about the role you want to project in your interaction and communication with other people. How do you want them to perceive you—your body language and tone of voice? Once you figure this out, then your mind will produce the visual expressions and vocal sounds to convey the meaning you wish to express.

In other words, when it comes to com-municating the image you project and the way you are perceived, you are not controlled or limited by what you have inherited from your parents. How you think and feel about yourself, the people you are with, and the situation you are in will determine your body language, the expression on your face and the sound of your voice. Relying on expensive clothes and cosmetics is no substitute for a clear confident voice, a warm smile, and a firm handshake.

12. Planning and Working:

PLAN YOUR WORK, AND WORK YOUR PLAN. BECAUSE WHEN YOU SUCCEED IN PLANNING, YOU ARE PLANNING TO SUCCEED.

Imagine driving to a city you have never been to without a map, GPS, or road signs on the highway. You will likely waste a fair bit of time and gas as you travel down various highways and run into unexpected detours. You will soon feel frustrated and test the patience of any passengers who are travelling with you. In short, if you don't know where you are going, how are you going to get there?

Ironically, when you fail to plan, you plan to fail. Luck and chance play a part in everybody's life, but you can't predict or control when or if they will occur. Prepared people often seem lucky, but planning helps you determine your objectives and take the appropriate steps required to achieve them. Opportunity is more likely to come to a mind which has been prepared.

You generally require seven resources to achieve your goals: people, time, money, space, information, equipment or tools, and energy. Devising a plan requires you to logically think through the sequential steps you need to take when using these scarce resources to achieve your objective.

Just as following a road map helps you confidently get where you want to go, planning will enable you to become more confident and reduce anxiety as you try to accomplish various objectives. If you naïvely believe you can't spare the time required to develop your plan, then where do you think you will find the extra time required to get back on track when you discover you are lost? Getting off course, or otherwise messing up on your way to your destination, will require additional time to get back on track or repair any damage caused by your failure to take the necessary time to plan.

Every minute you spend in planning and strategizing will save you considerable time in carrying out your plan. So, plan your work and work your plan. Don't do anything without first having a specific objective and a reliable plan in your mind.

Your plan represents your roadmap. It's how you get from point A to point B, efficiently and with greater confidence. So, as the American Express commercial says, "Don't leave home without it!"

13. Responsibilities and Relationships:

GOALS AND ROLES CLARIFY YOUR RESPONSIBILITIES; OBLIGATIONS AND EXPECTATIONS GUIDE YOUR RELATIONSHIPS.

Explorers in the past used compasses to help guide them through dangerous seas and unfamiliar terrain. Today, with satellites and advanced technology, we have a global positioning system (GPS) that can pinpoint specific locations with amazing accuracy.

Psychologically, there is a compass or GPS equivalent. It consists of four ideas, or concepts, which you place in your mind. Once you become aware of them and learn how to concentrate and focus on them, you will rarely become confused, insecure, or lost.

The psychological GPS is composed of goals, roles, obligations, and expectations. Your goals and roles identify your job and responsibilities.

Your obligations to and expectations of another person express the nature of this relationship.

Goals represent objectives you are striving to attain. Roles represent the functions and activities you engage in to achieve your goals. The combination of goals and roles clarifies the responsibilities or job you are required to do.

For example, in school, your role is student and your goal is to earn grades that will enable you to pass your courses. In a family, your role may be parent, spouse, son, or daughter. Your objective may be to develop harmonious family relationships. And finally, in a work setting, your role is that of an employee or manager. Your goal may be to ensure the success of the organization through the delivery of a product or service or through customer service and support.

Relationships are like bank accounts consisting of both deposits and withdrawals. In any relationship with another person, you have a responsibility to make it a positive and pro-ductive experience. This means you have some specific *obligations* to the person that you must meet to ensure the success of this relationship. This represents your deposits. But since all relationships are two sided, you also have some *expectations* of the other person that they should meet in order for you to feel satisfaction in your interactions with this individual.

To keep your bank account solvent, you have to put in more deposits that benefit the other person than take out withdrawals from the other person which solely benefit you.

Your list of obligations will likely resemble the other person's expectations; your list of expectations usually mirrors the other person's obligations. When discussed and agreed upon, obligations and expectations produce a 'relationship covenant' or relationship agreement based upon mutual respect, trust and collaboration rather than power, position or hierarchy. This covenant or agreement ensures that each person can hold themselves and the other individual accountable and facilitate greater synergy and teamwork.

When relationships and responsibilities are identified and agreed upon by individuals, you have a psychological GPS or compass that provides guidance, structure, and clear objectives. It helps keep people focused and working together in a mutually beneficial manner. And when people collaborate and respectfully co-operate, it ensures harmony and success.

In other words, harmony is not an accident. It is not based upon luck and chance. It is the result of choosing to behave as mature adults who are accountable for their relationships and responsibilities.

14. Setting Goals:

MOVING INTO THE DRIVER'S SEAT OF YOUR LIFE.

There is no such thing as a boring job, a boring marriage, a boring academic program, or a boring life. They are only as boring, or as interesting, as you are.

Boredom, curiosity, or enthusiasm starts within the mind and imagination. It develops from the simple act of setting goals.

If while playing basketball, the hoop is placed only one foot above the floor so the ball can simply and easily be dropped into the opening, the game will be very brief. The sense of achievement will not deliver any excitement or challenge. This will lead to apathy and boredom.

Conversely, if the hoop is placed twenty feet high, it will also be a brief game since the players will feel a sense of hopelessness and then give up in frustration.

Goals that are set too low result in boredom; goals that are set too high are perceived as unrealistic or unattainable and result in frustration and discouragement.

Goals should therefore be set just beyond your comfort zone so you have to stretch and extend yourself. Achieving something you had to work at leads to a sincere feeling of pride, satisfaction, and well-being. Unmotivated people rarely experience this sense of accomplishment because they are unwilling to 'endure the pain to achieve the gain'.

Boredom is, therefore, the result of your choices. When you accept the responsibility for establishing your objectives or goals in every situation, then you move into the driver's seat of your life.

Lewis Carroll, in his classic book, *Alice in Wonderland*, is famous for the quote: "If you don't know where you are going, any road will get you there." If you don't set your goals, other people will set *goals for you. Those goals will be in their best* interest, not yours. And so, the person with the goal is always in control.

15. Carpe Diem – Seize the Day:

GAIN CONTROL OF YOUR TIME, AND YOU WILL GAIN CONTROL OF YOUR LIFE.

Most of us have complained that we have too much to do or that we don't have enough time. But really there is no such thing as 'too little time' or 'not enough time.' The paradox of time is that although few of us seem to have enough of it, each of us has all the time there is. Every day contains the same number of hours for everyone—24 hours a day.

You cannot expand or contract time. A colleague who accomplishes more than you do does not have a 'special day' containing more hours than your day. Some people simply work smarter and use this scarce resource we call time more skillfully than others.

To better appreciate the power you actually possess when it comes to managing your time, simply remember how much you accomplished on the last working day before you took a few weeks of vacation. Or, conversely, recall how little time you had, or how little you actually accomplished when you were asked to do something you really didn't like or want to do.

Each of us has 168 hours a week. That amount of time may be insufficient to accomplish all of the things we need to do, or would like to do because we have an unlimited number of things to do, in a limited amount of time. In other words, work is infinite; time is finite.

Therefore, it is not the number of hours you put in that matters, but what you put into those hours. We are evaluated by the results we achieve and not by the time we spent to achieve those results. Or, as management expert Dr. Peter Drucker says: "Doing things right is not as important as doing the right things, for of what use is it to do the wrong thing, right?" This principle clarifies the difference between the terms 'efficiency' (doing the thing right) and 'effectiveness' (doing the right thing).

Without analyzing and understanding how you spend your time, you are at the mercy of "Parkinson's Law." It states that work expands to fill the time that is available. This means that if you have three hours to complete a task, it will usually take you about three hours to finish the job. If you analyze how you have spent your time over the past few weeks, however, you will be better positioned to determine how to choose your time expenditures in the future, based on your goals, objectives, priorities, tasks you can delegate, or personal preferences. You can also identify the time wasters and time savers that you and other people impose. They influence how productively you use your scarce time.

"Pareto's Law" is an indispensable tool that can be used to gain control of your time. This concept is also known as the "80/20" rule. In any list of things to do, 80% of the benefits can be derived from completing only 20% of the tasks; 20% of the benefits will come from completing the remaining 80% of the items. Applying Pareto's Law can help prevent you from getting bogged down and foolishly devoting your time to low value activities. By concentrating on the important 20% of any list of things to do—in other words, by focusing on the items that will deliver the highest payoff or benefits—you will end up working smarter rather than harder and longer.

16. Choose How You Think; Choose How You Live:

HARDENING OF THE ARTERIES DETERMINES HOW LONG YOU LIVE; HARDENING OF THE ATTITUDES DETERMINES HOW WELL YOU LIVE.

Most adults have a yearly physical exam with their family doctor to evaluate their general state of physical health. Very few adults, however, stop to consider the general state of their mental or psychological health.

For this assessment, no instruments, lab tests, equipment, blood or urine samples, or x-rays will be required. Answering ten simple questions will help reveal how well adjusted and successful you are in living with yourself and getting along with the people you interact with in your family, work, and social relationships.

Using a 1 to 10 point scale, with "10" meaning "Yes or Always", and "1" meaning "No or Never", please respond to the following ten questions to help determine your general state of psychological well-being.

Psychological Mental Health Quiz

1) Are you usually happy, satisfied, and content with how your life is going?

2) Do you have some enthusiasm, zest, energy, and passion for something?

3) Do you like being with other people? Do you enjoy interacting, participating and getting involved with people?

4) Do you have some sense of balance in your life? Does getting involved with a variety of things, such as family, friends, work and community, give you some satisfaction?

5) Do you successfully cope with setbacks and disappointments? In other words, do you constantly dwell on problems you had in the past and might have in the future?

6) Are you able to step back and objectively evaluate your own behaviour and actions, not just from your point of view, but from the perspective of others?

7) Do you have a trusting and confidential relationship with a few people that you respect and know you can confide in and count on?

8) Do you have a sense of humour? Can you laugh at yourself and not take yourself too seriously?

9) Are you engaged in a satisfying hobby, activity, pursuit, work, volunteering or learning opportunity that you enjoy?

10) Do you know how to *worry effectively*? Can you sleep through the night, even when you are dealing with an issue, and wake up feeling energetic and focused?

I suspect you know how to interpret your score. The closer you are to 10 for each question and the closer you are to 100 overall, the healthier you are psychologically.

With that in mind, let's take a closer look at some of the questions and implications of the questions. If you are inspired after reading the information below, you might want to take the quiz again.

1) Are you usually happy, satisfied, and content with how your life is going? If not, what are you doing to improve it? Just as a thermometer reveals that an increase in your body's temperature means you have a fever, so too general feelings of happiness and contentment mean you have made successful adjustments to your life.

2) Do you have some enthusiasm, zest, energy, and passion for something? A person who is curious and open to learning and change tends to be someone who looks forward to waking up each day to face the world so he or she can deal with its challenges and opportunities.

3) Do you like being with other people? Do you enjoy interacting, participating and getting involved with people? We are genetically programmed to be "social animals" and psychologically healthy people tend to enjoy interacting and getting involved with others in social, work-related, family and leisure situations. "Doers" usually have more fun than "Watchers".

4) Do you have some sense of balance in your life? Does getting involved with a variety of things, such as family, friends, work and community, give you some satisfaction?

Being a workaholic, or only having one thing you enjoy, is equivalent to putting all your eggs in one basket. When that basket breaks, you will find yourself at risk. A table can't remain erect standing on one leg. Our lives require diversity, various supports, and interests, if we are to avoid the dull monotony and boredom of constant repetition.

5) Do you successfully cope with setbacks and disappointments? In other words, do you constantly dwell on problems you had in the past and might have in the future? In short, are you a problem watcher, a problem creator, or problem solver? Can you skillfully deal with each problem in your life as it occurs? Do you know how to break big problems into smaller chunks so you can tackle them one piece at a time? Or do you take a lot of little problems, roll them together into a huge issue and then feel overwhelmed by the size of the mountain you have just created?

If you create mountains out of molehills or have difficulty dealing with issues one step at a time, consider subscribing to this clever poem:

Yard by Yard
Life is Hard,
Inch by Inch
Life's a Cinch!

6) Are you able to step back and objectively evaluate your own behaviour and actions, not just from your point of view, but from the perspective of others? It can be hard to objectively evaluate yourself. Sometimes trying to see yourself as others see you, especially others who might have been on the receiving end of anything you just said or did, can help you look at yourself more objectively. The goal here is to gain insight into your own conduct and understand why you act the way you do. If you are going to change, if you are going to manage and control your thoughts, impulses, emotions, moods and actions, you need that understanding first so you can better manage yourself, and therefore produce better consequences resulting from your actions.

Remember, "A person who is unaware is unaware that they are unaware." Without awareness, you are destined to simply repeat your past behaviour.

A broken finger in a cast will heal without your conscious cooperation. A cut on your body will form a scab and grow new skin without your help. Your hair and nails will grow without any effort on your part. However, your fears, anxieties, insecurities, jealousy, anger, sadness, resentment, bitterness, hopelessness, personality quirks, and so on will not improve without your active involvement. You need to decide to change how you think, feel, and behave before you can change those qualities. And you need to be aware of them before you can decide what and why to change. In summary, if you won't help yourself, then you cannot improve! A therapist can only help you help yourself. But they can't make the change on your behalf. Change is solely your responsibility.

7) Do you have a trusting and confidential relationship with a few people that you respect and know you can confide in and count on? For instance, are there a couple of people in your life who are reliable, will look out for your best interest, and are available to be there for you? If not, you may be isolated. You may be pushing people away. You have to open your heart and mind to let people in. When you let people who are good for you in, that makes for a psychologically healthier state. But sometimes you have to work on yourself, before you can open yourself to accepting others.

8) Do you have a sense of humour? Can you laugh at yourself and not take yourself too seriously? You can have fun without being frivolous, and you can be serious about some things without being unduly sombre. Being able to laugh at yourself is, fortunately, not a genetically inherited trait. It is something you can learn and develop. At the same time, you don't want to be so flippant that you can't admit to making an error and apologize. As well, you don't want to be so serious that saying "I'm sorry!" fills you with debilitating guilt and debases your self-esteem. You want to keep a happy, positive attitude and know when to have fun, when to laugh at yourself, and when to seriously address an important issue. In short, you want balance in all you do.

9) Are you engaged in a satisfying hobby, activity, pursuit, work, volunteering or learning opportunity that you enjoy? Passion and enthusiasm are signs of people with a sense of purpose and meaning. Seek challenges in your life that provide some sense of personal fulfillment and that help others too.

Centuries ago, Confucius said, "If you can find some work to do that you are committed to and that you can achieve at, then you will never have to work a day in your life." Samuel Goldwyn, the founder of MGM Studio, said, "No person who is truly enthusiastic about their work has anything to fear from life."

10) Do you know how to *worry effectively*? Can you sleep through the night, even when you are dealing with an issue, and wake up feeling energetic and focused? Chronic worrying causes sleepless nights, drains you of energy and focus, creates anxiety and in-decision and can make you a rather unpleasant person to be around. "Worrying effectively" motivates you to consider the cause of your concern, evaluate your available options and their respective pros and cons, and then mobilizes you to take action to correct or alleviate the source of your worry. In brief, "Don't stew. Do!" It's difficult to be depressed and active at the same time. But make sure the action you do take is constructive and useful.

Your choices for action usually fall into the three distinct categories:

- Start doing some things you have not yet been doing.

- Stop doing some things that are contributing to the problem.

- Continue doing the things you are doing that help eliminate the cause of your concern.

In summary, happy people and unhappy people frequently have similar problems. Successful and unsuccessful people usually struggle with the same issues. The crucial difference between these two groups of people has little or nothing to do with the specific nature of the problem itself. The main difference is the attitude (thoughts and feelings) individuals take when faced with problems and the actions, or in-actions, they choose to take when seeking a resolution.

If you attempt a course of action and it works out successfully, then your worry disappears and you feel elated, or at least relieved. If your actions don't produce the desired resolution, then you have learned that a particular approach doesn't work. Your worry or concern still has the same cause, so you can reanalyse the situation and try a different course of action.

The problem with doing nothing, and persisting with the same chronic worry and inaction, is that nothing changes. When you do nothing, and learn nothing, you remain stuck in the rut of your own creation. You get to choose. Learn by doing something, regardless of the outcome. Or learn nothing by doing nothing.

Things don't get better by chance. They get better by choice!

17. Choosing Rather Than Excusing:

"IF YOU THINK YOU CAN, OR CAN'T, YOU ARE RIGHT."
- *HENRY FORD*

Our habits significantly influence the failures and successes we experience in our life. We can change the habits we have learned by revising the thinking that developed and supported these habits in the first place. Outside of the traits we have inherited, we can change almost anything about ourselves. We can correct our mind and simply decide to become the type of person we actually want to become. In other words, just as we experienced a physical birth, which was the responsibility of our parents, so too can we experience a psychological birth, for which we are responsible.

Many of us develop excuses or self-defeating thoughts that limit our ability to achieve and succeed. These dysfunctional beliefs trip us up and get in our way. Some of the more popular excuses that we are all familiar with include:

1) Changing myself is very difficult.

2) Change will take too long.

3) Change is risky and there are no guarantees it will work, so why bother?

4) I can't afford to make changes.

5) I'm not smart enough or strong enough to change.

6) Nobody will help me, and I can't do this all by myself.

7) I'm too tired, old, or inexperienced to change.

8) *They* won't let me do this. It's probably against the rules.

9) It's not my nature to do this.

10) I'm too busy and I don't have the time to change.

11) I've never tried to do anything like this before.

12) It's impossible. If it was possible, somebody would have done it before.

13) It's too uncomfortable and will require more effort and time than I have available.

14) I'll get blamed or criticized if it doesn't work out well.

These self-defeating thoughts create barriers to our progress. In general, people do not attempt things they believe they cannot achieve. And so they seldom achieve more than they think they can. Or to quote Henry Ford again, "If you think you can, or can't, you are right." If you can't conceive it, and don't believe it, you will never achieve it!

As previously mentioned, a 10,000-pound adult elephant can be restrained by a chain attached to its leg even though it possesses the strength to knock over trees and snap the chain—as long as the chain was initially attached to its leg when the elephant was a baby. The real restraint is not the chain attached to the elephant's leg. It is the belief in the mind of the animal that limits its movement. Sadly, most of us have "chains on our brains" that have limited us in the past and continue to do so even though we possess the ability to break free of them. Instead, we allow these self-defeating excuses to continue to restrain our actions.

At times we are all underachievers. Most of the barriers we experience in life are psychological, not physical. The length of time it has taken us to develop a limiting habit is not related to the length of time it will take to change that habit. When we eliminate our self-defeating excuses, we will be able to move into the empowering position of "choosing rather than excusing." Albert Einstein affirmed this concept: "Imagination is more powerful than knowledge because there are no limitations on what our minds can conceive." Nobody has ever died from over thinking. But before you can begin to think creatively and constructively, you need to break the chains that bind you.

18. We Live in Our Minds:

"CHANGE YOUR THOUGHTS AND YOU CHANGE YOUR LIFE."
- *LAO TZU*

Lao Tzu, a sixth-century BC Chinese philosopher, came up with this "Change your thoughts and you change your life" concept many, many centuries before the field of cognitive psychology was conceived. Dr. Wayne Dyer has expressed this same principle in this way, "If you change the way you look at things, the things you look at change." In other words, all of our actions are the result of our choices. We are where we are today because of where our past thoughts and ideas have taken us. And, we will be tomorrow where today's thoughts lead us.

We carry in our head a mental map or paradigm that reflects the way we see, understand, and interpret our world. This perception of ourselves, other people and our present situation or circumstances becomes our reality. As Steven

Covey powerfully points out, if you want small changes, then work on your behaviour and habits. But if you want transformative changes, then work on your mental paradigms, or ways of thinking about yourself, other people, and the situations you are dealing with. In other words, each of us has two very clear options:

- An ineffective alternative: Believing that people are almost totally the product of their life's circumstances and that past thoughts and experiences will determine our present and future fate.

- An empowering option: To believe that people are primarily the product of their current life choices and actions and that even when it is impossible to change a situation it is still possible to change oneself to better adjust to the circumstance.

Our thoughts are expressed by our language, the words we use to convey our ideas. We can use Reactive Language or Proactive Language to conceptualize our response to any person or situation, as in the following examples:

Choice Points

Reactive Language	Proactive Language
There is nothing we can do about this.	Let's look at some possible alternatives.
He makes me so angry and upset	I control my own feelings.
I have to do this now	I will choose an appropriate response.
I ought (should or must) do....	I prefer to....

We always have the freedom to choose our responses to situations and events. Once we become aware of this, the realization changes everything. But, again, a person who is unaware is unaware that they are unaware. And so, in the absence of awareness, people generally repeat their past behaviours.

For most people, there is no genetic, biochemical or physiological basis for unhappiness, anxiety, stress, fears, anger, apathy, or self-pity. Although many people take pills or abuse alcohol to alleviate their so-called stress, there is really no such thing as stressful situations. There are, however, stressful thoughts about the situation, and that's what you can control.

We should never underestimate our power to change ourself. Choosing how we think will enable us to choose how we live. And it is this quality that makes us truly human.

19. We Live in the House We Build:

IT IS NOT OUR TALENTS, SKILLS, ABILITIES, OR TOOLS THAT MAKE THE DIFFERENCE IN THE RESULTS WE CREATE, BUT RATHER OUR INTENTION.

What is more important to our overall success in the accomplishment of our desired outcomes—the intention or desire we have, or the mechanisms or tools that we employ to achieve our desired outcomes?

While both our intention and the tools we use are important, nothing is more important than our desire and motivation. Having all the tools and resources to complete a task is useless if we do not have the desire. The tools we use are only as effective as the desire and skill of the person employing them.

There is a great story that illustrates this point. It is a story about a carpenter who was quite skilled and talented. After many years of building houses, and just before his upcoming retirement, he was asked to build one more house. He became complacent and lost his desire to pursue his work with excellence. On this last house he was building, he cut corners, paid little attention to detail and worked as quickly as possible to get the damn job done.

Since this was his last project and he was anxious to get it done, the carpenter did a horrible job. In short, this was the worst project of his career. Upon completion, his boss, the owner of the company, called him into his office and presented him with a set of keys.

His boss simply smiled and said, "In appreciation for your years of dedicated service, these are the keys to your new home. The house you have just built is for you!"

This story illustrates that each of us has to live in the 'house' we build. Our intention ultimately determines how we use what we have. Our intention is the most important factor in terms of whether we accomplish what we set out to do.

20. Mastering Recall – the Basis of Lifelong Learning:

REPETITION, ASSOCIATION, AND UNIQUENESS: THE KEYS TO MEMORY.

What good is learning anything if you are unable to remember what you have learned, where and when you need the information. A critical component of the learning process is memory. Imagine for a moment that you have mastered the ability to learn information quickly and easily; however, within a very short period of time all that you have learned was lost because you could not remember any of it, particularly at the times and places where this information was most needed. In this circumstance, having the ability to learn quickly and easily would have little or no value to you.

The most important aspect of developing your memory skills is mastering recall. You could have the most powerful computer in existence with the capability to store billions of bits of information, but, if you could not access this data when needed, it would be like having a vault with an abundance of riches and not having the key. It would be nice to have all those riches, however, the money is quite useless if you can't use it to purchase something.

The good news is that there are some simple strategies you can employ to recall information easily and effectively. While a vast amount of research has been conducted and many books have been written on this subject, when you distill the essence of effective recall there are three primary strategies you can employ to recall information more effectively. The three principles are Repetition, Association, and Uniqueness.

What gets repeated gets remembered. There is a rule of thumb that states "three times on the brain gets in the brain." So if you want to remember something better, encode the information into your brain three times, preferably in three different, multi-sensory ways. Tell yourself and/or someone what you want to remember. Write down what you want to remember. Draw a picture or symbol of the concept or thing that you want to remember.

Our memory is largely based on association. As we go through life, our brain is constantly linking or associating information, often in a random fashion. Association can also work in a multi-sensory manner. That is why hearing a song on the radio can sometimes evoke a distant memory of what you saw, heard or felt last time you heard the song. Use this principle to assist in recalling information by consciously associating what you want to remember with something else. Next time you park your car in a crowded shopping mall, consciously associate where you parked your car with a physical landmark. This will make finding your car easier when you return later in the day.

We also remember unique things, events, or circumstances. They may be different in terms of shape or form, odour, or taste, for instance. This is known as the Von Rostorff Effect. If, for example, you drove the same way each day back and forth to work, you would over time hardly remember one day's journey from the next. On the other hand, if one day while driving to work several elephants that had escaped from the circus crossed the street in the front of your car, you would undoubtedly remember for quite some time what happened, and when and where it happened. Incorporate this principle in order to assist in your recall by making what you want to remember stand out in some way. Try to associate it with an object or unique thought. Or simply type into the computer what you want to remember using a different colour so that you encode the information in your brain in a way that stands out.

Use the principles of Repetition, Association and Uniqueness to purposely imprint what you want to remember in your daily life so that you can recall this information later on, when you need it most. In short, use these techniques to access more of the genius that you truly are. Use it also to remember what you want to do, how you want to be, and the thinking you have to change in order to accomplish your goals. This will help keep you focused as you embark on your change journey.

21. You Can Only Really Change Yourself:

"BE THE CHANGE THAT YOU WANT TO SEE IN THE WORLD."
- *GANDHI*

The great contemporary author, speaker, and psychologist, Wayne Dyer, once stated the following: "Change the way you look at things and the things you look at change." He is also known for this insight: "If you are blaming the world for your problems, then you are going to have to send everyone on the planet to a psychiatrist for you to get better."

Whether we choose to accept it or not, the reality is that all change begins with ourselves. You cannot paint your living room by painting the outside of our house. And no matter how much you try, all the solutions you seek to your greatest challenges ultimately begin when you take personal responsibility for your life and look within.

It is far too easy to blame others, the economy, the weather, and a multitude of other external facts – events, circumstances, and conditions of our lives for the way we are. The truth is, in fact, the exact opposite. Our lives are a mirror of how we think, the decisions that we have made, and our beliefs and values.

Our thoughts and values may have been influenced by others, but it is only when we recognize that we are in charge that we can begin the process of shifting our awareness and begin to change. In other words, the world just "is" and it is through our thinking that we define how we want to shape our world.

Too often we wait, struggle, lament, complain, judge, or criticize when we have the power to shape and control ourselves and our thinking in relation to external circumstances. No one has said this more eloquently than Gandhi, who urged: "Be the change that you want to see in the world."

So how can we change our lives for the better? There are numerous ways that this can be accomplished. It all begins with changing our thinking.

Choice Points

Decide that you are in charge of your life. Begin to shape your internal world by taking direct and full responsibility for your life and circumstances. Continually feed your mind with empowering thoughts and ideas. Read personal and professional development books, listen to empowering CDs, or watch informative DVDs that will provide you with excellent methodologies, strategies, and techniques to positively influence your thinking and, ultimately, your reality!

22. How Decisions & Choices Shape Your Life:

"ONCE YOU MAKE A DECISION, THE UNIVERSE CONSPIRES TO MAKE IT HAPPEN."
- RALPH WALDO EMERSON

We have been given a great gift: the power and ability to decide how we would like things to be. Regardless of the current circumstances of our lives, we have the inherent ability to create our lives the way we want. Although the majority of our behaviours, learning, and changes that we make occur at a subconscious level, we can consciously decide to do things differently. For many people, this occurs at a point when they feel, due to external circumstances, that there is no choice but to move in a different direction. However, the reality is that, at all times, we have the ability to decide. Rather than simply being on auto pilot and reacting to the influences of the outside world, we can take control. Those truly in control of their lives and, ultimately, their destiny, turn the subconscious or unaware reaction into a conscious or aware choice. They choose how they want things to be and bring what they want into existence.

If you stop for a moment and think about it, the way your life is right now is largely a reflection of the choices that you have made up until this point. The great philosopher and poet Ralph Waldo Emerson often refers to the law of cause and effect as being one of the most powerful laws that shape our lives. This largely stems from the choices and decisions that we make.

Your past does not have to dictate your future. Like the law of gravity, the law of cause and effect is always at work and operating in your life, whether you believe it or not. Given this truth, one of the best decisions that you can ever make is to decide to make better decisions for yourself and your life.

Begin right now and decide to positively shape and enhance every aspect of your life, including your health, relationships, and economic prosperity. It is generally easier to start with small decisions, such as deciding to eat more healthy meals. Then, through your success in shaping your eating habits, you can move up to larger decisions and watch how your circumstances, and indeed your entire life, start to improve for the better.

It all begins with you and your power to make wise decisions and choices!

"Shallow men believe in luck, believe in circumstances. Strong men believe in cause and effect." – Ralph Waldo Emerson

23. Create Your Best Possible Future Now:

CREATING YOUR IDEAL FUTURE

With your every thought you are creating your future. Most people are unaware of the incredibly powerful role that their thinking plays in shaping and defining their future. The average person often has one random thought after another based largely on what is occurring in their external environment and on what has occurred in their past experiences and conditioning.

This process of reacting to an external stimulus results in repeating similar experiences to the ones we have had in the past. While the people around us and the circumstances we are in may change, most of us are creatures of habit. We simply replicate the past repeatedly by running unconscious programs created from our past life experiences. These programs run in the background; we simply go on autopilot.

We have learned how to do many behaviours, such as how to walk, without consciously thinking about them because our brains have this ability to automate and habituate our behaviour. For the most part, having this ability serves us well as it frees us to engage in multiple tasks simultaneously and to learn new things. Without this ability, we would have great difficulty getting anything done. Imagine if you had to think about how to walk every time you needed to get somewhere. A problem arises, however, when our past behaviour no longer serves us and we want our present or future reality to be different. The same behaviours that, in the past, served a useful purpose can prevent us from realizing our full potential in life.

We have within us, however, an incredible, largely untapped, power to create the future— not as it has been based on our past but rather how we want it to be based on our new thoughts. The key is to turn a largely uncon-scious process into a conscious one, a process that involves using how your brain creates reality with volition, or by using your will.

Your brain is most often involved in six things: seeing pictures (reading is your brain seeing and interpreting pictures known as letters), hearing, feeling, tasting, smelling, and generally ruminating about what you are experiencing through your five senses. If you are not doing at least one of these things right now, immediately check your pulse to see if you are alive!

One of the absolute keys to creating a brighter and different future, one that is different than your past, is to project or imagine your ideal future using the six activities our brain can engage in. You do this in a way that enables you to project, then create, your future exactly as you want it to be. When you create a future experience for yourself using all your senses, you are overriding the past default conditions and providing your brain with a new program to run based on your desired outcome.

Most traditional goal setting teachings, while powerful in their own right, tend to typically use the visual sense by having the person project a visual image of their desired future. While powerful in its own right, this technique has its limitations. When you involve all your senses in your projection, however, you dramatically increase the power of generating what you want. This happens, in large part, because our past memories are comprised of all five senses and our self-talk. In the cortex of the brain there is considerable overlap in our sensory memories, which means we have different memories for each one of our senses. This is why, when you hear your favourite song on the radio, it often evokes sounds and feelings. It may even evoke images, smells, and tastes that are associated in our memory with the song.

Given that the brain involves all our senses in making up our memories, and the fact that our brain cannot distinguish between a real or imagined experience, we can use this process to create our desired future reality. In essence, you can use what your brain is doing naturally to great benefit.

So how do you do this? The first step, as with setting any desired outcome, is to decide exactly what you want to create for yourself in the future. Every goal should conform to what is commonly referred to as the 'S.M.A.R.T.' criteria:

> **S** = Specific
>
> **M** = Measurable
>
> **A** = Achievable

R = Relevant

T = Timeframe

Specific:

Define in specific terms what it is that you want to create (as opposed to what you do not want or what you want to avoid). Make sure what you want is within your power to create and not dependant on the actions of others.

Measurable:

Define the evidence for having achieved your desired outcome. What has to occur to indicate that you have achieved your desired result? (What will you see, hear, smell, taste, and/or feel?)

Achievable:

Write your goal down as if you have already achieved it, i.e., "I have..." or "I am..." Again, make sure what you want is within your power to create, not dependent on the actions of others. The goals have to be realistic and within your capacity to achieve.

Relevant:

The goal has to be relevant and appropriate to your situation.

Timeframe:

Goals require a metric and a specific completion date for their accomplishment.

Represent the last step as having accomplished your desired outcome in a multi-sensory way. In other words, represent your future goal vividly in your mind, as if you have already accomplished it. What will you see, hear, and feel when you have achieved your goal? Let go of any doubts, limiting beliefs or negative thoughts that may come up by focusing on what you want to do instead.

Trust in the process. Just as when you plant a flower seed in the garden, you don't continually dig it up to see if it is growing. Once you set a future goal, you do not need to continually check the process. Remember, things take time. Feed your future with positive thoughts, feelings, and actions; then allow the process to take its course. Once you have set things in motion, perhaps the most powerful thing you can do is to let go and trust the process.

Once you have defined your goal in accordance with the SMART criteria, you then create a rich vivid mental representation of your desired outcome. Imagine that you have already achieved your desired outcome. What do you see, hear, feel, smell, and taste? What are you saying to yourself about your experience?

The more you can step into the experience, as if it were happening now, the more you will be programming yourself towards your future experience, in your mind.

What you are doing, in essence, through this process is proactively using your brain to create the best possible future for yourself based on how your brain actually works. You are, in short, taking conscious control over what would otherwise happen in a largely unconscious manner. By doing this, you are in the driver's seat of your life experiences rather than letting unwanted past conditioning dictate your future. The more you do this consciously and with volition, the more desirable and enjoyable your future reality will ultimately be!

If you think this is not possible, then how will you make it possible? If you think this is not possible, then you are letting past conditioning interfere with the future reality you want to create. If you want this to be possible, change the way you think.

24. Ten Ideas to Stimulate and Enhance Learning:

PRACTICE MAKES THE LEARNER, NOT PERFECT, BUT BETTER.

Here are ten ideas to help stimulate and enhance your learning:

1) **Reinforcement**

Learners usually repeat behaviours that are rewarded, sincerely acknowledged, and positively reinforced or commented on. Similarly, criticism, punishment or other feedback that reduces the learner's sense of self-esteem reduces the positive impact of learning. Learner behaviours that are ignored or receive no positive or negative reaction often diminish in frequency, unless there is a particularly strong meaning or purpose in the mind of the learner for repeating the behaviour or retaining the learning.

2) **Emotional Learning**

If the material to be learned has some strong emotional relevance to the learner, then the information or experience will be retained for a considerably longer time, sometimes even for the rest of the person's life. Learners often forget exactly what an instructor or mentor says or does, but they seldom forget how they feel. That emotion, if strong and powerful, can serve to lock in the memory of the information that was provided.

3) **Practice and Feedback**

Learners generally do not master the skills or information being taught if they have no opportunity for repeated practice, combined with immediate feedback and coaching. Practice makes the learner, not perfect, but better. Continuous practicing over time develops "performance habits" and once something is a habit, it can be repeated when, and as may be, required.

4) **Active Learning**

Participation, active involvement, group and individual presentations and other active learning activities produce more effective learning and retention than passively listening or reading. As well, doing something is usually more enjoyable than simply listening or watching. In addition, people become more committed to things they create, rather than to something that somebody else has imparted.

5) **Relevance**

For learning to be effective, the material must be relevant and meaningful to the experience and life of the learner. The learner has to be able to relate to the information and see themselves in some way connected to what is being discussed. Therefore, learning should be more problem—or issue—centered rather than subject-matter centered. This allows the material and learning experience to be more in sync with the needs, concerns, and interests of the learner.

6) **Individual Differences**

Each learner comes with a unique combination of strengths and weaknesses, preferences and styles of learning and interacting with other people. Plato, in his classic book *The Republic*, was the first person to acknowledge the concept of "individual learning differences." Different people learn and behave in different ways. Both the teacher and the learner need to be aware of what style or methods work best for the learner and then capitalize on this information to enhance the effectiveness of the learning process.

7) **Previous Experience**

The attic of a house cannot be built before the basement and lower floors have been constructed. Similarly, new learning should be linked to and built upon previous learning and experiences of the learner. New learning will be better absorbed if the learner better comprehends the background and context of the new material. Ignoring this recommendation is like throwing a beginning swimmer into the deep end of the pool without the swimmer having acquired the skills of staying afloat and, perhaps, actually swimming. Previous learning enables the learner to be more psychologically secure and confident of success when they are presented with new challenges, material, and experiences.

8) **Self Direction**

Adults are used to solving problems, taking initiative, and figuring out what they need to do to achieve their goals. Learning should build on these abilities. Most adults are self-directed learners, especially when it is expected, encouraged, and positively reinforced. They are responsible for so many other aspects of their lives that learning just naturally becomes one more challenge and opportunity. Being spoon fed and treated with condescension will often lead to withdrawal of the learner, either physically or psychologically. Being respected, engaged, and empowered releases energy, creativity, and motivation, which produces results often beyond the expectations of the learner and teacher.

9) Self Image

Adults bring with them to the learning process their self-concept, self-esteem and general sense of identity. This has been developed over many years of participating in learning experiences. Their perceived success or failure in the past contributes ideas that can either interfere or enhance their current and future learning. Being accepted, respected and encouraged by a caring and competent mentor can break a previous negative pattern and open the door to new levels of achievement.

10) Learning from Each Other

The formal leader or teacher is not the only resource for teaching and learning. Every participant has valuable experiences and ideas that can contribute significantly to the learning process. Time and opportunity, however, must be made available for their contributions to be encouraged and provided. In addition, when colleagues cooperate, share experiences, learn, and teach each other, they form a bond of caring and affiliation that extends beyond the original learning environment and the lessons provided by their formal teacher.

25. Ten More Ideas to Stimulate and Enhance Learning:

LEARNING PLUS APPLICATION EQUALS CHANGE AND PROGRESS.

Here are ten additional ideas that will help stimulate and enhance your learning:

1) DISCOMFORT

Learning can sometimes become a painful process as the learner is encouraged and challenged to move out of their "comfort zone." As the often quoted expression puts it, "No pain, no gain!" When new information is presented, the learner is often required to respond and perhaps change or abandon previous ways of thinking, feeling, and behaving—especially in the presence of other people. When that occurs, there is always the potential for embarrassment and defensiveness. Fear of failure, and perhaps criticism or negative feedback, can stimulate emotional reactions that make it more difficult to be open and receptive to the benefits of this new information or new way of behaving. The interpretation of change can either be viewed as "danger" or "opportunity", so one's attitude to his or her sense of discomfort plays an important role in how new learning is accepted.

2) **EXPECTATIONS**

How someone enters a learning experience is primarily their responsibility. How they leave this experience is primarily the responsibility of the teacher, mentor, or coach. The reaction of learners to the learning process is significantly influenced by their expectations of and attitudes toward the leader, the content, the methods and style of instruction, the inter-actions with fellow participants, the importance and relevance of the learning opportunity as perceived by the learner, the sponsoring organization, and so on. These all combine to either enhance or detract from the learning experience.

3) **MULTIPLE CRITERIA**

Different people use different standards or criteria to evaluate their learning experience and accomplishments. The instructor or coach might employ quantitative assessments; the learner might use comparisons with peers, personal progress since the last evaluation, or even enjoyment of the learning process. In short, there are a variety of methods that can be used to assess any activity, depending on the individual's objectives, previous experience, and the use to which this evaluation will be put. In answer to the question, "How would you evaluate 'X'?" the answer could be, "Compared with what?" Is the judgement a relative or absolute measure? What is the impact of the evaluation? The evaluation method or criteria employed should be stated up front, prior to the beginning of the learning process, so there are no surprises and unintended negative conesquences that will provoke emotional, defensive reactions on the part of the learner.

4) **ALTERNATIVES**

In the field of mathematics, there is only one correct answer. Ten plus four, for the rest of human history, will always total fourteen. But in many other endeavours, there are several ways of doing things. We are fallible human beings and, therefore, do not possess perfect knowledge (omniscience) or perfect control (omnipotence). Consequently, we will initially make some errors as we learn any new material or new way of doing anything. The learning environment must provide opportunities for the learner to try new ideas and approaches and explore alternatives presented by the participants or teacher. It must also support responses that don't match exactly what the teacher or book of instructions endorses. In other words, it must not humiliate, reject, or punish the learner for exploring. These negative consequences reduce the learner's motivation to learn and experiment or to create new ways of dealing with the material presented by the instructor.

5) **INVOLVEMENT**

Meaningful learning requires action on the part of the learner. Mastering skills and acquiring knowledge increases to the extent that the learner is invited and obligated to participate. The learner should be able to ask questions and should be challenged to respond to questions posed by the instructor. In addition, learners should share and contribute their views throughout the entire learning process. Interacting with the teacher and one's fellow participants also enhances the general level of enjoyment and satisfaction the learner experiences in the learning environment.

6) OWNERSHIP

People become committed and supportive of the ideas and objects they help create. Learners have a stronger motivation and resolve to implement their own concepts and values rather than those of others. Because of personal ownership, most of us occasionally wash and polish our car; we seldom do the same with an automobile we have rented for the weekend. Similarly, we are motivated to make our own bed, but seldom do we make up the bed in a hotel where we have just stayed for the night. Pride of ownership is key to implementation!

7) ALIGNMENT

Learning is strongly enhanced when the training objectives, content of the material, method and activities in the instruction process, as well as the evaluation techniques and criteria, are all aligned and mutually supportive of each other. Focused energy has more power than energy which is dispersed and not concentrated or aligned.

8) REFLECTION & FLEXIBILITY

Without thoughtful reflection, there can be no real learning. And if there is no new learning, then there can be no change. Without change we are in danger of becoming irrelevant and failing. Therefore, being flexible, open, and receptive to new ideas, along with a willingness to move outside of our comfort zone and an ability to reflect on what we have learned, guarantees our adaptability, relevance, and success.

9) DEMONSTRATION

The only way learners can truly prove that they have learned something is when their behaviour—what they actually say and do—demonstrates it. Learning can't be assumed to have happened on the basis of blind faith. To establish the credibility of the learning process, the student must be able to consistently show they have mastered the skill and acquired the knowledge. When they can repeatedly do this, they will be able to develop new habits that they can apply as may be required or desired.

10) $L \times A = C = P$

Learning x Application = Change = Progress

Learning, without applying what was learned, is a wasted learning opportunity. If the learning is not put into effect, than the learner is no better off than someone who did not attend the course or workshop. Similarly, continuing to apply only what was previously learned, and not acquiring any new learning, is a recipe for maintaining the status quo. Mathematically, on a scale of 1 to 10, the equation would look like this:

Learning x Application = Change = Progress

$10 \times 0 = 0$ Change = 0 Progress

$0 \times 10 = 0$ Change = 0 Progress

But 10 x 10 = Great Change = Great Progress

The purpose in learning anything new is to use it to enhance and improve the situation.

In brief, learning allows one to make a positive difference!

26. Do, Learn, Repeat with Improvements:

DO THE RIGHT THING AND YOU CAN SUCCEED. DO THE WRONG THING AND YOU CAN LEARN FROM THE EXPERIENCE. DO NOTHING AND YOU WILL SURELY FAIL.

More problems develop through errors of omission (doing nothing) rather than errors of commission (doing something). When you do something and it has positive results, you learn that the strategy will likely be successful again, and you tend to repeat it. If your approach produced a negative outcome, you will likely not repeat it. And so doing something, even if the consequences are not what you hoped they would be, produces the benefit of learning.

Doing nothing, however, produces no positive outcome and no opportunity for learning and improvement. Doing nothing means you learned nothing. Therefore, you are no wiser the next time you are presented with a similar issue or problem.

As long as a life experience does not kill you, you can learn from it regardless of whether the result was positive or negative. So when faced with a situation, seek a positive outcome. But if uncertain, take what you feel is appropriate action and learn from any errors you might make.

27. Don't Try; Do:

"DO OR DO NOT. THERE IS NO TRY."
- *YODA*

The word 'try' is a weasel word. It indicates you would like to be evaluated only on the basis of your motivation and effort, and not on the basis of the actual results you achieved.

Imagine boarding an airplane and asking the pilot, "Will you land the plane safely?" How would you react if the pilot answered, "I'll try!" Most of us would likely get off the aircraft because we would not have confidence in the pilot's skill, experience, and confidence.

Similar phrases such as 'strive', 'I guess', 'perhaps', 'attempt', 'intend', 'hopefully', 'maybe', 'have faith in me', etc., all imply doubt, luck, and chance rather than confidence in positive results and success. These are all words that deny personal accountability and responsibility for one's actions and the conesquences that follow. You want assurance and commitments, not evasions and hedging, when you ask people if they can do something. It's safe to say others expect that of us.

In truth, there is no 'try'. You either do it, or you don't do it. You either will, or you won't. The road to hell is paved with good intentions, as the saying goes. If the individual you are counting on displays a lack of confidence and uncertainty about the results of their efforts, why should you have more confidence in them than they have in themselves?

People rise and fall in relation to their expectations of themselves. Weasel words provide the clue as to the amount of confidence and effort the other person is prepared to invest and commit.

The difference between people who are more successful, and those who are less successful, is not generally the amount of information or knowledge they have, but rather their commitment to action. You cannot distinguish between smokers and ex-smokers by the amount of health knowledge they possess. The ex-smoker uses the knowledge and information about the consequences of smoking to quit smoking. The smoker possesses the same health information about smoking but doesn't apply the knowledge to make the necessary changes in their behaviour. And so a knowledgeable smoker is no better off than an uneducated smoker who is unaware of the negative consequences of smoking.

To know and not do is to not know. Therefore, avoid 'trying' and resolve to simply 'do.'

28. Errors and Mistakes:

THE DIFFERENCE BETWEEN AN ERROR AND A MISTAKE IS MOSTLY A MATTER OF ATTITUDE.

Since we can't know everything, and can't do everything, it is obvious that we will make errors. We can screw up with any person, in any place, on any project, at any time. If we actually possessed omnipotence and omniscience, and never made errors, we would be god-like, rather than human, and there would be no need for improvement.

If you make an error, you should "A-A-A-A": *Acknowledge* it, *Accept* responsibility (rather than blame others), *Apologize*, and *Act* to fix the situation. And then, learn from the experience so you don't repeat the error in the future.

If you keep on making the same mistake, then you can't attribute doing so to not possessing the appropriate knowledge. The same mistake made repeatedly is the result of defensiveness or an unwillingness to change, rather than an incapacity or inability. This negative attitude, even if it is a self-protecting one, changes an accidental error into a deliberate mistake.

Deliberate mistakes, even if we are unconscious of how we are sabotaging ourselves or a situation, are the result of dysfunctional and self-defeating attitudes. Our emotional reactions, defensiveness, and ego get in the way and transform accidental errors into deliberate mistakes. Accidental errors can be fixed and, through learning, avoided in the future. Deliberate mistakes that might be tolerated by others will likely continue to be made. Perhaps they will even get worse in the future, unless someone steps in and forces us to change our action.

Accept accidental errors in yourself or others, and learn from them. But do not tolerate mistakes!

29. Pain, then Gain:

YOU HAVE TO PASS THROUGH DIFFICULT TO GET TO EASY.

Remember the several times you fell as you learned how to rollerblade or ride your first two-wheeler? Most of the important lessons in our lives that have been meaningful and have helped us develop our skills were not quickly learned; most were learned with some pain, too. Effort, persistence, patience, motivation, false starts, and plain old hard work and resilience were required to move from a state of awkwardness to a feeling of comfort and mastery. The adage that "Rome was not built in a day" is just as true today as when the expression was conceived.

For everything to be clear and simple and to work out quickly, easily and successfully, we would have to be Superman or Wonder Woman. We would have to be people possessing perfect knowledge (omniscience) and perfect control (omnipotence). This god-like state is not possible for fallible human beings like us, and so we have to accept the concept of 'no gain without some pain.' Contrary to popular belief, practice does not make us perfect. But practice, and the learning that accompanies it, can make us better.

And so we end with this motto: 'Quitters never win; and winners never quit.'

30. Thermometers and Thermostats:

THERMOMETERS ARE PASSIVE AND MERELY REPORT THE TEMPERATURE; THERMOSTATS HAVE GOALS AND ARE CHANGE AGENTS. BE A THERMOSTAT.

A thermometer is a passive instrument that accurately records the temperature of your body or some external environment. A thermometer simply describes an event or situation. That's all it does. It reveals how hot or cold something is. It reflects what is, but has no power to change or influence the status quo.

On the other hand, a thermostat operates as a change agent, helping to make something warmer or cooler, or even keeping it constant, depending on what is needed to make the environment more suitable according to some previously established criteria.

To develop and manage yourself, and to significantly influence your environment and other people, you have to choose to be a thermostat. As a thermometer you simply accept the way things are and feel no responsibility to help improve either yourself or the environment in which you live. As a thermostat, you become a continuous agent of change, sensitive to what's needed for maximum performance and minimum disruption.

If you operate as a thermometer, people will rarely remember that you were even there. You will have no track record and you will have left very few positive memories of achievement. You will not make much of a difference.

Being a thermostat is much more demanding as you will feel obliged to meet the continuous challenges of daily life. You will never be bored or completely satisfied. You will likely shake people out of their complacency and ruffle a few feathers, but you will also have had a more rewarding and fulfilling life as you leave behind a positive legacy that will be remembered because you will have made a significant difference.

31. Your Space; Your Responsibility:

HOW PEOPLE ENTER 'YOUR SPACE' IS THEIR RESPONSIBILITY. HOW THEY LEAVE IT IS YOURS.

People may come into 'your space'—office, classroom, factory floor, home—with either positive or negative feelings, moods or emotions. They bring their own thoughts, expectations, values and previous life experiences all wrapped up in their heads.

But what happens in your space is significantly up to you. You can guide the discussion and its tone, mood and outcome. You are not obligated to react or to allow yourself to be controlled by their priorities. Your choice of how you initiate or respond in the discussion is based on your clear understanding of your role and the objectives the other person and you have for this interaction and relationship.

Before a conversation begins, you have to eliminate previous thoughts. You must shut down the last telephone call, email, or project you were working on. The way you remove a thought in your mind is to replace it with another thought. It's like replacing a CD or MP3 file with a new one if you wish to hear different music.

Prior to meeting the person in 'your space', simply ask yourself this question: What is my role with this person, and what are my goals for this upcoming discussion? (Remember, the person with the goal is always in control.) If you refuse to establish an objective, you will likely be manipulated or swayed by the person who possesses a specific reason or goal as to why they want to meet with you.

Make people feel welcome. Give them the attention and respect they deserve. Listen to their information and point of view and share yours in a calm and rational manner. Solicit, and be receptive to their feedback, and equally share yours. Let them leave 'your space' with the feeling that they have had a fair and honest discussion with you. And make sure that there's no confusion about what you and they need to do next. If it helps clarify roles and responsibilities, end your meeting with a reiteration of who does what next, when, where, and why.

Over time, the person will likely forget much of what you have said or done, but they will not forget how they felt about the interaction they had with you. Emotions last longer than your words or actions.

32. Focus on What You Want to Create:

ASK YOURSELF, "WHAT DO I WANT?"

We are extremely creative beings. Moment to moment, day by day, month by month, year by year and throughout our lives, we are constantly creating our present reality and cir- cumstances. Most of us are unaware of the fact that we are largely the cause of our life circumstance; many of us do this totally unconsciously and without direct deliberation and intention.

Our thoughts are extremely creative. Before most things in the material world came into existence, they first were created in the imagination of our mind. When an artist paints a remarkable painting, he has painted it twice: once in his mind, and a second time on canvas. Most of the things in the general vicinity of where you are right now were first thoughts in the minds of people prior to their creation and manifestation in the material world.

While we are constantly creating our reality and bringing into existence the events and circumstances of our lives, all too often we bring into reality what we don't want either by default or because our focus is on what we want to avoid instead of on our intended desire.

A good example of this occurs on race tracks. Some drivers, in attempting to navigate very tight turns, hit the wall and crash while others are able to make the turn without spinning out. Taking into account environmental conditions like weather and track conditions, one of the key determinates as to whether a driver crashes or safely makes it around the turn is their focus. The drivers who crash invariably were focused on not hitting the wall; the drivers who safely navigated the turn were focused on where they wanted their cars to go.

The life lesson here? Instead of focusing on what you do not want, or do not want to happen, focus on what you want and how you want things to be instead. The principle here is simple. We get more of what we focus on because what we focus on has a greater probability of becoming reality.

There is a powerful principle of neurophysiology that goes a long way in explaining how this works: the brain cannot process a negation. In other words, if I were to ask you to *not* think about a "purple tree" you would first have to think about the purple tree in order to not think about it. The same principle is at work when we focus on what we do not want. Instead of creating what we truly want, all too often we get the opposite of what we want. We get what we were attempting to avoid.

So, as you think about what you want to create in your life, state your outcome in the positive. Instead of thinking I want to avoid going into debt, think of all the ways you can create wealth. Instead of thinking about how you don't want to get into car accident, think about how you will arrive safely at your destination.

In order to easily apply this principle, there is an important question that you can ask yourself whenever you find yourself focusing on what you do not want. Simply ask yourself: **"What do I want?"** This is a powerful question because it forces the mind to refocus your thinking from an undesirable outcome to the desired result, a result that you truly want.

In summary, we get more of what we focus on, so focus more and more of your thoughts, feelings, and actions on what you do want and you will get more and more of what you want more and more of the time!

33. Pursuing Excellence:

PERFECTION CAUSES CONSTIPATION.

Do not confuse perfectionism with the pursuit of excellence. Excellence places a premium on quality, reliability, consistency, and high standards of effectiveness.

Perfectionism is a neurotic attempt to achieve the unachievable. It is fuelled by an obsessive and compulsive need to achieve 100% no matter what you are doing, where you are doing it, when you are doing it, or with whom you are doing it.

The need to achieve perfection immobilizes the doer. Since it cannot be achieved, other than in rare circumstances, it discourages enthusiasm, energy, and the attainment of any degree of sustained joy and satisfaction.

This pursuit of perfection results in never being pleased with yourself or the achievements of anyone else. It eventually destroys relationships and the desire of other people to cooperate with you since you are never satisfied with their efforts or your own.

Attention to detail is important, but per-fectionism—creating "paralysis by analysis"—is a painful way to live. You might say that perfectionism causes a kind of psychological constipation!

Achieving 40% of a worthwhile goal is better than trying to achieve 100% of an objective that is impossible to achieve. Going into a situation feeling you have to be perfect will cause you to procrastinate. You may never even get started, let alone invest the effort required to attain your goal. Something is better than nothing! So strive to do well, but there is no need to feel you have to do it perfectly.

34. True Competition:

COMPETE WITH OTHERS AND YOU MAY WIN THE DAY; COMPETE WITH YOURSELF AND YOU WIN FOR LIFE.

When there is internal competition in a classroom, workplace, or family, people avoid sharing, helping, and supporting each other. Teamwork, collaboration, and coop-eration disappear as each person vies for attention and their place in the spotlight. The law of the jungle replaces mutual self-interest and the concept of interdependence and synergy. In a co-operative situation, 1 + 1 can equal 3 because the whole can be greater than the sum of its parts.

The measure of success is not whether you were smarter than Einstein, or more musical than Mozart. These comparisons pit you against world-class experts and you are doomed to feel inferior. Instead of asking yourself how you measure up against external sources, there are fairer and more reasonable questions to ask. How can I use the talents I have? Did I leave situations worse, about the same, or better than they were? Did I make a positive contribution and difference?

Over the long run, in relationships that promote winning and losing, everyone ends up losing something as people greedily hoard resources and refrain from working together as a team. This type of internal competition in an organization often allows external competitors who *do* work as a team to win every time.

When team members in a family, work or school setting are encouraged to co-operate with each other and to strive to improve upon their previous performances, relative to the demands or requirements of the situation, they tend to do their best each day. In such situations, people find themselves on a lifetime path of winning continuously. And, that is a race worth competing in!

35. Visible and Verbal:

PEOPLE WHO DON'T SPEAK UP,
RARELY OFFER THEIR OPINION,
AND GENERALLY REMAIN
SILENT, WILL NEVER BE
MISQUOTED. BUT THEY WILL
ALMOST ALWAYS BE
MISUNDERSTOOD.

The old saying that 'silence is golden' may still work for undercover agents and spies, but it's a recipe for disaster in building effective, mature relationships.

People who are quiet and say very little naïvely believe that people can read their minds and know what they are thinking without them having to speak up. In the absence of information, people make assumptions which are frequently wrong. The biggest error you can make in communications is to assume you have achieved it! Shy, quiet people rarely request or provide comments, questions, or feedback, which makes two-way communications and transactions difficult to initiate, let alone maintain.

Communication skills rank right at the top in every successful person's toolkit. Teamwork and meaningful dialogue are impossible with passive bystanders. You not only have to be visible, but you also have to be verbal. This means sharing, clarifying, asking questions, providing answers, explaining and offering, and requesting feedback. With over 5,000 spoken and written languages, and with the English language containing almost one million words, the human voice can convey meaning and emotions superior to the most complex piece of technology.

But to overcome your silence, you have to believe that you have the right, as well as the responsibility, to share your views. If you are an introvert, that requires you to step outside of your comfort zone and speak up! And if you are an extrovert, it may require you to concentrate on listening or giving those around you an opportunity to speak up, because communication is a two-way street and all parties involved in an issue need to speak up and listen, for communication to be effective.

36. Winners and Losers:

LOSERS LOOK FOR A COMMON ENEMY; WINNERS LOOK FOR A COMMON GOAL OR SOLUTION.

Think about how many of your friends and colleagues spend a lot of time telling you why something won't work. They see the negative side of virtually everything somebody else proposes and they become trapped by their self-made walls of pessimism, cynicism, and defeatism.

Their negativity stifles enthusiasm, creativity, energy, and teamwork. They hide from the real challenge of seeking ways to eliminate barriers that get in the way of reaching objectives and seem to forget that it's a lot more satisfying to resolve a problem than it is to wallow in one.

People generally fall into three broad categories: problem watchers, problem creators, and problem solvers. Your learning, progress, and general life satisfaction will more likely be assured if you strive to be a problem solver and you surround yourself with other problem solvers.

Losers build walls that separate and divide people as they focus on common enemies they are trying to protect themselves from.

Winners build bridges that enable people to communicate and interact as they focus on common ground and goals to promote their mutual interests and solutions.

37. Respect, Trust, and Cooperation:

YOUR TITLE GIVES YOU AUTHORITY, BUT IT IS YOUR DEMONSTRATED BEHAVIOUR THAT ACTUALLY EARNS YOU RESPECT, TRUST AND COOPERATION.

Your title, position in the organizational chart, sign on your office door, business card, certificates on the wall, where you sit in a meeting, and so on, all reveal some measure of your status, influence, and power and establish some indication of your authority—what you are entitled to receive in terms or remuneration and how other people should interact with you.

In older times—in ritualistic, religious and tightly structured cultures or organizations— these lines of authority and hierarchy clarified what behaviours between people were appropriate. But in our North American society, in the 21st century, this rigidity has been replaced by a more fluid and flexible method of human interaction. Age, gender, socioeconomic status, experience, and education no longer control the manner in which, and the extent to which, people interact and cooperate with you. Previously, respect and trust could be commanded. Now they have to be earned. Blind obedience can no longer be assumed.

In today's organizations and society, empowerment, assertiveness, sharing of scarce resources, participation, speaking up, mutual responsibilities, and teamwork all require collaboration and cooperation. Although the parent, teacher, or boss may have good intentions, and may evaluate themselves based on those intentions, the child, student, or employee is not able to assess the intentions of another person because intentions cannot be seen or heard. We only know they exist when they are demonstrated by the other person's actions and behaviour—what they actually say and do on a consistent and habitual basis.

If there is a discrepancy between what the person with the title and authority preaches and what he or she practices, between their rhetoric and the reality of their actions, then they are described as "not walking their talk." They are viewed as hypocritical and not functioning as a credible role-model. Respect, trust, and cooperative behaviour are diminished when people perceive that you don't lead by example.

Although we may judge or evaluate ourselves on the basis of our intentions, we evaluate other people, and they in turn assess us, on the basis of the specific behaviours that are demonstrated. Again, intentions cannot be seen or heard. Only actions can.

With that in mind, when you habitually connect your intentions with your actions, when you actually 'walk your talk,' you will gain something valuable: personal integrity. Having a sense of personal integrity will lead to enhanced self-esteem and increased respect, trust, and cooperative behaviour. Who could ask for anything more?

38. Perception is Projection:

WHEN WE CHANGE OUR PERCEPTIONS, OUR PROJECTIONS CHANGE AND OUR EXPERIENCE OF REALITY AND LIFE CHANGES.

Many people operate with the incorrect assumption that the world outside is independent of their thoughts and perceptions. They believe that the world, society, the economy, the day-to-day reality of existence is separate and apart from how they think. Many simply react to external events and circumstances as if they have little or no ability to affect them in any way. These people operate on the effect side of the 'cause and effect equation' by simply assuming that their thinking about the outside world has little or no impact on what happens to them and what they experience.

The world and the reality that we experience is a reflection of our internal thoughts and feelings. Therefore, what becomes real is what we think and feel! We project our thoughts and feelings onto the external and this, in turn, colours how we experience life.

Reality just is. How we see reality, however, is very much a function of how we think about it. As Shakespeare masterfully wrote, "Nothing is either good or bad, but thinking makes it so." Similarly, the philosopher Nietzsche wrote that there are no facts; there are only interpretations and opinions.

If you are having a bad day and your thinking is negative, this profoundly impacts how you interact with others and how they treat you in kind. The same is true if you are having a good day and your thoughts, feelings, and actions are positive. The assumption many people make is that how they are treated and what happens in their lives is outside their control or unrelated to them. Often times people feel victimized by the very circumstances they themselves played a major role in creating. When we take direct responsibility for our thinking and operate from the cause side instead of the effect side of the equation, everything changes for the better.

The good news is that with an understanding that the external world is a large mirror of our internal world, we can control how we think, feel, and behave. By changing our thinking, we literally change our whole experience of life. When we change our perceptions, our projections change, and our experience of reality and life changes.

So, rather than be a victim of external events and circumstances, take back control and choose the most optimal way of thinking about the world and what you want your life to be like. Project the best for yourself and what you perceive over a period of time will become what you experience as reality!

39. Congruency of Thought and Action:

THE WORLD JUDGES YOU BY WHAT YOU DO, NOT BY WHAT YOU THINK AND SAY.

Very often we judge ourselves by what we think and say to others. The world judges us, however, not so much by what we think and say, but rather by what we actually accomplish and do. When we are congruent or consistent, our behaviour is in alignment with our thoughts and statements.

Many people think great thoughts and say great things about what they intend to do or not do. At first, the people whom we interact with take us at our word. When our actions do not match what we say about what we will do, however, over time people lose confidence in our ability to follow through. This results in a loss of credibility and respect. Important relationships in our lives, the relationship we have with ourselves and our self-esteem, suffer.

Do consistently what you say you are going to do. If this means promising less and doing more, then all the better. There is a great saying: "Under promise and over deliver." When you do this, not only will your thoughts, statements, and actions be congruent, you will earn the respect and admiration of everyone with whom you interact. The result is better and more harmonious relationships, increased self-esteem and confidence, and a rock-solid belief in your abilities.

When we believe in ourselves, backed up by a proven track record of aligned thought and action, we will have put in place the foundation for even greater accomplishments. Greater opportunities will then come to us because others will trust that we will do what we say we will do. This will form a great cycle of positive expectations and become the basis of lifelong success and accomplishment.

40. Your Mind, The Greatest Resource:

TAPPING INTO THE INCREDIBLE POWER OF YOUR MIND.

Of all the resources we have as human beings, both tangible and intangible, the most powerful resource we possess is our mind. As human beings, we are blessed with an immensely powerful and unique gift: the ability to think and to craft and shape our destiny with our thoughts.

Everything that has ever been created began at first as a thought. This is an inspiring notion when you consider the magnificent inventions that have been developed, all the way from the great pyramids of Egypt to the Hubble telescope. Today, we live in a world where there is a seemingly endless stream of innovation. And all of our past, present, and future innovations are initiated from a single source: the mind.

We all have within us the ability to tap into this awesome power that can be used to shape our lives and to enhance the development of humanity itself.

However, for many people, this incredible power lays dormant as we allow our lives to be profoundly influenced by external circumstances or by the thoughts, opinions, and limiting belief systems of others or by our own lack of self-confidence.

Like the elephant that has been tethered to the pole since childhood, we are often unaware of the ability that we actually possess to break free of the limitations of the past by thinking differently. One of the greatest gifts that you can give to yourself, and indeed the world, is to begin to learn about, explore, and ultimately tap into the powers of your mind. By doing so, you can truly make a positive difference in your own life and in the world. Now it's up to you to become aware of this capacity and learn how to use it.

41. Acquiring the 5 R's:

THE 3 R'S ALLOW YOU TO GRADUATE FROM HIGH SCHOOL; ACQUIRING THE 5 R'S ENABLES YOU TO BE SUCCESSFUL IN LIFE.

Literacy and numeracy expertise were colloquially referred to as "Reading, Writing, and 'Rithmetic." These skills enabled you to be promoted from one grade to the next, ultimately ending up with a high school diploma.

Knowing how to read, write, and deal with numbers is a basic requirement for employment, but so much more is needed to keep your job or to be successful in your voyage through life.

The 5 R's represent the fundamental building blocks of a successful career and mutually satisfying interpersonal relationships at home, with friends, at work, or at school. The 5 R's below are not arranged in order of priority; however, the absence of any one of them will diminish your opportunity to be effective in your relationships with other people.

1) **RESPECT**

In the past, your title, age, position, tenure, education, or family background were used to establish your formal authority and power to influence other people. Today, we no longer automatically bestow that recognition and credibility upon people. We focus on the individual's demonstrated behaviour and actions as the basis for our esteem and respect. We look at the person's habits—what they say and do, and how they say and do it—before determining the respect we will bestow upon them.

In the past, respect could be commanded. Now it has to be earned! And, we are only as good as our last performance or deed. Respect has to be continuously earned to establish our reputation, but it can be lost in an instant by some type of non-sanctioned or socially unapproved action.

The benefits of gaining respect are enormous. When somebody respects you, they will trust you and generally cooperate fully with you. The absence of respect usually leads to minimal compliance or co-operation and substantially less commitment. Not practicing what you preach, or not "walking the talk", is perhaps one of the fastest ways to lose respect.

Respect for other people begins with respect for oneself. When respect is present in relationships, caring, compassion, and love are allowed to flourish!

2) RATIONALITY

We have a choice. We can behave emotionally or rationally. When we *react*, our feelings, moods, and impulses determine our actions. Our thoughts about what is more appropriate become secondary. However, when we *respond*, we consider our options and choose our behaviour based on the present situation, our goals, and standards of conduct that we believe to be suitable. This means that we can develop an internal compass, or GPS, that will guide our actions according to some rational plan and objectives.

3) **RELATIONSHIPS**

We are programmed genetically to be social animals. We choose to associate with other people and much of our life's satisfactions are derived from positive interactions with family members, friends, work or school colleagues, and people with whom we share some common interests or values.

Relationships are similar to bank accounts. You have to deposit more than you withdraw. You have to give more and take less to create a viable relationship in which both parties benefit. When this occurs, you have created the magic of synergy in which $1 + 1 = 3$, or in which the whole is greater than the sum of its parts.

In our complicated, interdependent world, productive relationships are essential because we rarely do anything that does not involve other people.

4) **RESPONSIBILITY**

The word 'responsibility' could be expressed as 'respond with ability'. As mature adults, we have to accept the fact that we are responsible for the choices we make and the actions that stem from these choices and decisions.

In each waking moment, we choose our thoughts, our feelings or emotions, and the behaviours or actions that we commit. But we do not get to choose the consequences. The consequences choose us.

Although our parents are responsible for our birth, we are responsible for our life. We accept the fact that we are responsible for filling our car with gasoline when the gauge nears "empty" because the automobile cannot fill itself up. We are also responsible for drinking when we are thirsty, eating when we are hungry and putting on a sweater or jacket when we are cold. And so, if we are responsible for our physical well-being, we must also be responsible for our mental or psychological well-being. We can choose *not* to become angry, moody, lazy, or impatient. We can also decide to become more friendly, cooperative, patient, and caring. The choice is up to us and the consequences of our actions are either positive or negative.

If we don't want the negative consequences to occur, then we should anticipate what the likely results will be before we say or do anything. Once we determine the results we want, we can choose to change our behaviour in light of our goals, to increase the probability that we will achieve positive consequences or results. When we do this, then we are truly "responding with ability."

5) **RESILIENCE**

There is no shame in falling down. The shame is in not attempting to get back up and trying again. In baseball, you have three strikes before you are called "out." But in life, you have many opportunities to try again. And yet many people give up when their first effort does not produce the results they had hoped for.

There is an old adage that is appropriate here: "Quitters never win and winners never quit." So flunking an exam, having a marriage end in divorce, failing in a business venture, not landing an audition, and so on, only means that this particular effort did not produce the positive results you desired. Most home runs in baseball are not made on the first swing, but on the second or third swing. Babe Ruth, the "King of Swat," had more strike outs in the same year he hit a record number of home runs.

Failure is never permanent unless you decide not to try again, and only you can make that decision. Thomas Edison, the world-famous, prolific inventor literally failed hundreds of times before he successfully created the electric light bulb. Albert Einstein failed in high school mathematics and is now regarded as perhaps the most brilliant person of the last century.

Perhaps Eleanor Roosevelt offered the best advice about resilience when she said, "Nobody can make you feel inferior without your permission and cooperation."

Keep going. Don't quit.

42. We Live in the Age of the Mind:

SHAPE AND DEFINE EVERY ASPECT OF YOUR LIFE.

As a society, we have evolved from living off the land in an agricultural-based economy, to an industrial economy, to an information-based economy. We are continuing to evolve to what is now being referred to as the Age of Mind Power.

This is a state where we have the majority of our subsistence needs met by modern day inventions which have, in turn, freed us to focus on the most powerful resource that we have: the power of our minds. In large part, this is why change is occurring at such an exponential pace.

With the obvious exception of our vast oceans, there are two areas that mankind has yet to fully uncover: the secrets of the cosmos and the mysteries of the human mind. According to some researchers, these two worlds are deeply interconnected.

One of the greatest discoveries of the 20th century was made by the University of London Physicist David Bohm and Stanford University Quantum Physicist Karl Pribram. Although largely unknown, these scientists discovered that both the human brain and the entire universe operate like a hologram. They concluded that our thoughts influence and play a profound role in shaping our current reality. With this discovery, modern day science has validated what man has understood on a largely intuitive basis for centuries.

Just as we now know that the mind and body are deeply interconnected, so too is the mind and everything else that we experience. This is an incredibly liberating and empowering notion. By learning about and discovering the powers of your mind and by using these powers with direct intention, you can literally shape and define every aspect of your life. No longer are you limited by past ways of thinking and conditioning, or the limited beliefs and thoughts of others. You truly have the ability to create, be, have, and do what you desire in life.

Choice Points

There is a great universe of possibilities that exists within each of us.

43. Mastering Ambiguity:

IT IS IMPORTANT TO TAKE RISKS IN LIFE AND TO FEEL COMFORTABLE ACTING IN UNCERTAIN SITUATIONS.

One of the most important skills we can learn is how to master uncertainty and ambiguity. In all spheres of life, rewards go to those who can thrive in unpredictable environments. In organizations, the members who are compensated the most are those who have to make decisions where the outcome is uncertain. Take a bank for instance. The bank CEO's compensation is many more times than that of a bank teller. There are many reasons for this related to the differences in knowledge, experience, and education between the CEO and the bank teller. However, one of the major differences is the degree of ambiguity that each must deal with in the execution of their daily work.

The CEO has to make decisions that can have a profound impact on the financial fortunes of the bank, its employees, and investors and, indeed, on the overall economy. Bank tellers, on the other hand, follow set procedures in the execution of their daily work and, as a consequence, deal with little ambiguity.

In quantum physics, there is a powerful principle called the Heisenberg Principle. It states that we will never have all the knowledge and information we require to make any decision with absolute certainty. In short, despite all our efforts to prepare ourselves for anything, there will always be an element of unpredictability and uncertainty as to the outcome and consequences of our actions.

We simply have to learn how to feel comfortable acting in ambiguous and uncertain situations and environments.

The only real security we have is what we give ourselves in coping and dealing with change. It is the confidence we place in our ability to take action and to respond to the unpredictable events and circumstances that inevitably arise. Each of us has managed our life up until this point, dealing with all the twists and turns that life brings, and we have survived.

Choice Points

One of the greatest ironies in life is that when we give up the need for complete certainty and control, and put our trust in our ability to influence our future and successfully respond to situations, we can then move confidently forward and accomplish many of our dreams, goals, and desires.

44. Focus on Service to Others:

ONE OF THE KEYS TO SUCCESS IN BUSINESS, LIFE, AND OVERALL PERSONAL AND PROFESSIONAL HAPPINESS, IS TO FOCUS ON PROVIDING SERVICE TO OTHERS.

Many people don't ever think of providing service to others. Whether it is in their business or personal lives, many people view the world from the perspective of what they want, what they need, or what's important to them. However, serving the wants, needs, and aspirations of others can lead to greater business and personal success.

The irony is that if all you do is focus on yourself you will never be as happy, successful, and prosperous as you will be by focusing on serving others. This may seem counterintuitive; however, it is very true.

In a business, the salesperson who only defines their world by how many sales they can make, or how much money they can earn, will never be as successful as the sales rep who cares for the needs of clients and focuses on how much service they can provide.

One of the major sources of misery and unhappiness is when a person is completely self-absorbed and solely focused on their own problems and concerns. It is when we dedicate ourselves to serving others that we are able to escape self-imposed limitations.

It has been said that "giving initiates the receiving process." When we give of ourselves, our time, our knowledge, our talents and skills, we set in motion a causality chain of events and circumstances that comes back to us in many positive ways.

"Giving is better than receiving because giving starts the receiving process." – Jim Rohn

"I have found that among its other benefits, giving liberates the soul of the giver."
– Maya Angelou

45. Appreciation and Gratitude:

WE TEND TO FORGET THAT
HAPPINESS DOESN'T COME AS A
RESULT OF GETTING
SOMETHING WE DO NOT HAVE,
BUT RATHER OF RECOGNIZING
AND APPRECIATING WHAT WE
DO HAVE.

- FREDERICK KOENIG

Most of life's greatest truths are really quite simple. One of these is the concept of appreciation, which is the recognition of the quality, value, and significance, of people, things, ideas, and life itself.

In our hectic lives, few of us take a moment to stop to consider how very fortunate we really are. It is easy to get caught up in thinking about what we do not have or the goals that we have yet to accomplish. We often fail to consider the many blessings that daily enrich our lives. We are alive, we live in a part of the world with abundant resources, and most of us are in reasonable health.

In life, we get more of what we focus on. When we concentrate our thoughts and attention on what we lack and our limitations, we seem to experience more lack and limitation. On the other hand, when we focus our thoughts and energy on the many positive aspects of our lives, more good shows up.

The mere act of appreciation, of being grateful for all we have and have accomplished, is a catalyst that enriches our lives and brings more good into our lives.

It has been said that a "truly wealthy person is someone who simply appreciates what they have." Even if you had all the money in the world, great relationships and perfect health, all this would be worthless without a deep sense of appreciation and gratitude.

46. Miracles:

"THERE ARE ONLY TWO WAYS
TO LIVE YOUR LIFE. ONE IS AS
THOUGH NOTHING IS A
MIRACLE. THE OTHER IS AS
THOUGH EVERYTHING IS A
MIRACLE."
- ALBERT EINSTEIN

If you think your life is not something special
and absolutely magical, consider this quote
from Stephen Hawking in *A Short Cut to a
Miracle*:

*"Approximately 15 billion years ago our
physical universe came into being in an
explosion of absolutely incomprehensible force.
At the moment of this great cosmic explosion,
searing hot energy that had been compressed
into an atom was released— enough energy to
form all the matter that exists in the universe
today. This too was incomprehensible.*

*Planet Earth is part of the Milky Way Galaxy, a
cluster of some two hundred billion stars. The*

span of our Galaxy is 100 thousand light years (to figure out how many miles that is multiply 100 thousand by 6 trillion). We now know that there are thousands of Galaxies within 100 million light years from us and billions of others within the range of our telescopes and the universe is still expanding. Some of these Galaxies are one billion light years away and moving away from us at a speed of 100 million miles an hour. The most astonishing thing of all is if within one second of the moment of the beginning, the rate of expansion of cosmic energy had been different by plus or minus one part per quadrillion, you and I would not be here today. One part per quadrillion less and the universe would have blown apart too fast for the Galaxies and the stars to form. One part per quadrillion more and the universe would have collapsed in on itself before life could have evolved. In either case we would not be here and neither would anything else."

When we get caught up in our day-to-day subjective struggles and challenges, it is far too easy to forget or simply be unaware of how truly miraculous it is that you and I are here in the first place. In cosmological terms, the span of our life is but a mere blink of an eye. When one considers how special and indeed miraculous it is that we are here in the first place, one can easily believe that each of us has a unique and special responsibility to make the very most of our existence.

In practical terms, each of us has been given a unique, special and rare gift—the gift of life itself. As such, in our own way, we must define how best we can acknowledge, appreciate, and give back to the universe for this gift. For most of us, if we are extremely fortunate, we may have 100 years or so in this life. We may not have chosen to be here in the first place; however, we are here and perhaps the greatest gift that we have is our ability to choose what we want to do with the time we have. How we make the most of this precious gift that is nothing short of a miracle.

47. Please. And, Thank You.

COURTESY IS TO RELATIONSHIPS AS OIL IS TO MACHINERY.

Two of the most important phrases in our vocabulary need to be 'please' and 'thank you'. It's not just children who have to learn and practice these life lessons; it's everyone, everywhere, and on every occasion, with everyone.

Remember how you felt when somebody took you for granted and simply ordered or demanded that you perform some activity or complete an assignment that had an impossible deadline. Asking for cooperation, making a reasonable request, and starting your communication with the word 'please' makes the relationship warmer, more respectful, more courteous, and, yes, more human and mutually satisfying. It also increases the level of the person's cooperation and performance.

Choice Points

After the completion of a task, courteous people should then remember to show their appreciation by expressing a simple and sincere 'thank you'. Every time an individual acknowledges someone's contribution, four important benefits will occur:

1. People will realize that they matter, that they're valued as a person, and that their work has made a difference. Feeling important and appreciated makes people feel better about themselves.

2. As a person, you'll feel better about yourself for recognizing this contribution and feel proud of your own empathy and interpersonal skills.

3. A bridge—or bond—will form, or become stronger, between you and the person you're thanking, and there will be more warmth and mutual respect in the relationship.

4. Because of this positive reinforcement, that person is more likely to engage in similar behaviour in the future.

Think of it this way: performance that is acknowledged with sincerity gets repeated. There is no cost, other than a few moments of your time. Yet the benefits are boundless for the person, for your team, and for you.

Courtesy, when it becomes habitual, significantly enhances personal and working relationships and builds a stronger team to deal with future challenges and opportunities. So consider courtesy.

Please.

And, thank you!

About the Authors

The Book Club, from left to right:
Robert Reaume, Harvey Silver,
Phil Hollander

Phil Hollander

Phil is currently the Director of Professional Development for the Morris Real Estate Marketing Group, where he designs and delivers seminars throughout both Canada and the United States. In the past decade, Phil has delivered several hundred seminars to thousands of professionals in the Real Estate Industry.

Phil first became interested in learning and how the mind works in 1981 when he attended the Society for Accelerated Learning Techniques conference at IOWA State University. At that conference were gathered the world's most prominent brain researchers who were, and still are, at the forefront of what has become to be known as the Accelerated Learning Movement.

Throughout his career, Phil has custom-designed training and development programs for Fortune 500 companies throughout North America. He has also been a keynote speaker for many associations and organizations and has taught professional development seminars for Atkinson College, York University.

Phil has an Honours BA from York University and a Master's Degree from Brock University.

Robert Reaume

Bob has had a distinguished 40-year career in the advertising media industry. Beginning with media buying and planning at Ronalds-Reynolds Advertising in Toronto, he subsequently served in media and research positions at the Bristol-Myers Company as well as the Global Television Network.

In addition to this corporate work and establishing his own consultancy, Reaume & Associates, Bob garnered extensive experience with industry trade associations. He has served as President of the Outdoor Advertising Association of Canada and the Canadian Outdoor Measurement Bureau, as well as Executive Assistant to the President of Global Television. He is currently the Vice President of Policy and Research at the Association of Canadian Advertisers in Toronto.

Bob holds a Bachelor degree in English from York University in Toronto, and an advertising diploma from St. Clair College in Windsor, Ontario.

Dr. Harvey Silver

Harvey is an Organizational Psychologist and Human Resources Management Consultant with 35 years of professional experience helping thousands of people promote and practice better mental health in the workplace. He is the only psychologist to have served as a Director and Vice President of the Toronto Better Business Bureau.

Harvey has a Ph.D in counselling psychology from the State University of New York and has been an Associate Professor of Adult Education at the University of Toronto. Harvey has conducted seminars, conferences and workshops with over 700 organizations in North America, including one third of the *Financial Post's* 100 Best Companies to Work for in Canada. Because of his broad experience, he was selected by Maclean's Magazine as one of the 'top Human Resources consultants' in Canada.

Harvey effectively stimulates people to challenge and extend themselves beyond their comfort zone so they can become more successful in dealing with themselves and the people they interact with at work and at home.

.

CPSIA information can be obtained at www.ICGtesting.com
Printed in the USA
LVOW12s0341011113

359325LV00005B/18/P

9 780988 122703